KEEP IT
SIMPLE !!

Relish
SCOTLAND

Original recipes from Scotland's finest chefs and restaurants. Introduction by chef Geoffrey Smeddle.

First Published 2018
By Relish Publications
Shield Green Farm, Tritlington,
Northumberland, NE61 3DX.

Twitter: @Relish_Cookbook
Facebook: RelishRestaurantGuide
Instagram: Relish_Cookbook
For cookbooks and recipes visit:
www.relishpublications.co.uk
For publishing enquiries visit:
www.relish-publishing.co.uk

ISBN: 978-0-9934678-7-5

Publisher: Duncan L Peters
General Manager: Teresa Peters
Design: Vicki Brown
Proofing Coordinator: Valerie McLeod
Relish Photography: Nicky Rogerson
Editorial Consultant: Paul Robertson
Twitter: @paulrobbo1966

Front cover photograph by: Nicky Rogerson,
KG Photography, www.kgphotography.co.uk

Printed in Poland on behalf of Latitude Press

Relish
PUBLICATIONS

Welcome to this fourth edition of Relish Scotland, with a mouth-watering collection of recipes from Scotland's finest chefs and restaurants. We know you will enjoy cooking your way through the pages of this beautiful guide.

Since starting Relish Publications in 2009, we are privileged to have worked with hundreds of talented and highly acclaimed chefs, some of the biggest names in British food, and now have a national portfolio of over 29 regional, fine-dining guides and bespoke recipe books.

We have circumnavigated the UK in our hunt for the most highly acclaimed eateries, hidden gems and those highly recommended by other top chefs in the UK.

As the proud owner of a Relish cookbook you can also subscribe for a free Relish Rewards Card which entitles members to exclusive offers at some of the featured restaurants, ranging from a bottle of Champagne to free gifts when you dine.

We love to hear from our readers! Why not post your culinary efforts on our Facebook or Instagram pages? And, if you have any questions for the chefs, email our friendly team - marketing@relishpublications.co.uk.

So, next time you're planning to dine in an outstanding restaurant or cook for friends, tantalise your tastebuds with one of our beautiful books, lie back and think of England, Scotland or Wales and enjoy planning your next meal!

Best wishes and bon appétit  x

004
CONTENTS

006
CONTENTS

Scallops, Cauliflower, Raisin Puree - **Page 200**

009
STARTERS

Bouillabaisse with Hake & Local Shellfish - **Page 182**

011
MAINS

013
DESSERTS

015

FOREWORD BY GEOFFREY SMEDDLE

It is no secret that Scotland's larder offers produce that is the envy of chefs across Britain. Scotch beef, lamb, seafood, soft fruits, wild mushrooms and wild game, are but a handful of the products which provide inspiration to restaurants throughout the land. They represent the vital foundation to Scotland's thriving and diverse culinary scene.

The glorious pages which follow are a passionate expression of Scotland's contemporary restaurant culture, bursting with inspiration and offering a seductive invitation to discover some of the country's top chefs.

But who can write about Scottish chefs and their restaurants without turning to the supporting cast of producers, growers, farmers, fishermen and suppliers? These unseen and unsung heroes are the real stars. Where would chefs be without them? A successful dish relies perhaps on 80 per cent the ingredients and 20 per cent the chef. Whether you are looking to recreate some of the following recipes or trying to decide which of the restaurants in this collection to add to your bucket list, Scottish ingredients will undoubtedly be central to the experience. And that is surely something for everyone to relish.

Geoffrey Smeddle, The Peat Inn

016
21212

3 Royal Terrace, Edinburgh, EH7 5AB

0131 523 1030 or 0345 22 21212
www.21212restaurant.co.uk

As they approach their tenth birthday, 21212 remains a firm favourite within the Edinburgh dining scene. Paul Kitching's unique dining experience is a performance that people from all over the world flock to enjoy. From the cryptically named dishes to the artistically designed dishes, Kitching's 21212 creates a dining experience to remember.

"Katie and I had been spending our holidays in Edinburgh some 10 years before we actually opened 21212.

"During those years we massively enjoyed its August Festival but sort of secretly hoped, dreamed and yearned that maybe, one day in our own futures, we'd open a restaurant together in Edinburgh. The serious food scene and culture in Edinburgh made the challenge even scarier," says owner Paul Kitching.

"Hey presto, and now it's been almost 10 years since we actually opened our dream restaurant. The 21212 'thing' was a big move and commitment for us. We have the most beautiful restaurant in the most beautiful Georgian townhouse in the most beautiful Royal Terrace you could ever imagine.

"The work is hard and it's scary but boy is it wonderful and worth all things," enthuses Paul.

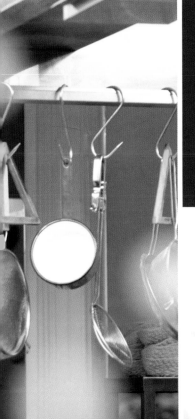

"Hard work has blessed us here at 21212, the most beautiful Georgian town house controls everything we do, it's in charge, not us. It's magical and demanding!"
Paul Kitching.

HAGGIS (HA-GUESS) IT'S RISOTTO

SERVES 4

 Kalecik Karasi, Kayra, Anatolia
(Turkey)

Ingredients

HP Mayonnaise

50g HP sauce
100g mayonnaise
1 tbsp stock syrup

Aubergine Purée

1 aubergine
1 bulb garlic (peeled, crushed)
100ml water
50g vegetable trimmings
salt and pepper (to season)

Onion Compôte

1 white onion (*julienne*)
4 tbsp olive oil
1 tbsp white sesame seeds
1 tbsp black sesame seeds
1 tbsp cumin seeds

Risotto

300g pudding rice
300ml cream
400ml stock
1 clove garlic (finely diced)
50g onion (finely diced)
salt and pepper
2 tbsp olive oil

To Finish The Risotto

150g haggis (grated)
200g Isle of Mull cheddar (grated)

To Serve

selection of soft vegetables (steamed pak choi,
mushrooms or shallots)
4 tbsp muesli
olive oil (drizzle of)

Method

For The HP Mayonnaise (Prepare ahead)

Mix all the ingredients together and store for later use.

For The Aubergine Purée (Prepare ahead)

Preheat the oven to 100°C.

Dry roast the aubergine until soft, about 2 hours.

At the same time, heat the water and soften the garlic and vegetable trimmings.

Once the aubergine is soft, dice and add to the garlic and trimmings. Cook out for 1½ hours, then blitz and pass through a sieve. Season and save for later.

For The Onion Compôte

Add all the ingredients to a pan with a lid and cook slowly on a low heat, occasionally stirring, until soft, about 2 hours.

For The Risotto

Add all the ingredients to a pan and cook until the rice is *al dente*. Once the rice is cooked, stir in the haggis and cheddar.

To Plate

Put a dot of the HP mayonnaise in the bottom of each dish with some onion compôte resting on top.

Reheat the risotto, vegetables and aubergine purée. Place the risotto on top of the compôte, then arrange the vegetables on top of the risotto.

To finish, add some of the muesli, a drizzle of olive oil and aubergine purée.

Chef's Tip

You can prepare all elements of this dish in advance and carefully reheat prior to serving.

CHICKEN, FIG, ARTICHOKE

SERVES 4

🍷 *Pinot Noir 'N' 2012 August Kesseler, Rheingau
(Germany)*

Ingredients

Artichoke Sauce

5-6 Jerusalem artichokes
½ lemon (juice of)
water (to cover)
butter (knob of)
1 shallot (finely sliced)
600ml chicken stock
100ml double cream
salt and pepper (to season)

Chicken

4 chicken breasts (skin on)
salt (to season)

Vegetable Garnish

1 Romanesco cauliflower
8 new potatoes
1 small turnip
4 large radishes
mangetout (handful of)

To Serve

20ml olive oil
2 slices black pudding (halved)
4 dried figs (rehydrated in vegetable stock)

Method

For The Artichoke Sauce (Prepare ahead)

Wash, peel and cut the Jerusalem artichokes into cubes. Reserve in lemon juice and water.

Melt the butter in a pan and sweat the shallot over a low heat.

Add the artichokes when the shallots are translucent and sweat for another 2 minutes. Pour in the stock and cream, simmer gently for around 30 minutes or until the artichokes are easily pierced with a knife. Blitz and season to taste, reserve. Reheat for serving.

For The Chicken

Preheat the oven to 70ºC.

Season the chicken with salt and dry bake in the oven for 45 minutes. Once cooked, remove from the oven and loosely cover with a cloth.

For The Vegetable Garnish

Wash all the vegetables thoroughly. Cut the Romanesco into florets, the new potatoes into quarters, the turnip into triangles and the radish and mangetout into diagonally cut halves. Cook, all separately, in salted, boiling water.

To Serve

Heat the olive oil in a frying pan and cook the black pudding. Remove from the pan and turn the heat up. Brown the chicken breast, skin-side down. Add the figs to heat through when the chicken colour is almost correct.

In a separate pan, gently reheat the vegetable garnish with a splash of water and olive oil.

Serve and cover with hot artichoke sauce.

POTTED CHOCOLATE, SHORTBREAD

SERVES 4

 Verdicchio Passito 2015 Bambule, Marche (Italy)

Ingredients

Rhubarb Compôte And Purée

5 rhubarb stems (cut into 3cm pieces)
200ml stock syrup
100g rhubarb purée

Chocolate Pots

45g egg yolks
42g caster sugar
300ml double cream
65g milk chocolate

Orange Chocolate Anglaise

60ml double cream
60ml whole milk
30g orange flavoured chocolate drops
23g egg yolks
22g caster sugar

Burnt Chocolate Drops

8 orange flavoured chocolate drops
8 white chocolate drops

Chocolate Shards

30g orange flavoured chocolate drops
30g strawberry flavoured chocolate drops

Shortbread

50g butter
25g sugar
75g plain flour

Chunky Cottage Cheese Cream

35g cottage cheese
15g natural yoghurt

To Serve

cocoa powder
icing sugar
popcorn

4 mini ceramic troughs
4 espresso cups

Method

For The Rhubarb Compôte And Purée

Cook all the ingredients slowly until thick. In a blender, blend half of this mixture until smooth to make the purée.

For The Chocolate Pots

Preheat the oven to 98°C.

Pour a layer of rhubarb purée at the bottom of each of the ceramic troughs. Beat the egg yolks and sugar. Bring the cream to the boil and add the chocolate, then slowly pour the mixture over the yolk mixture and combine. Pass through a sieve and pour the liquid on top of the rhubarb purée. Place the troughs into a roasting pan and add water up to three-quarters of the dishes. Bake for 30 minutes.

For The Orange Chocolate Anglaise

Heat the cream and milk until bubbles start to form, then add the chocolate drops. While the cream is heating, beat the egg yolks and sugar. Slowly pour a little of the hot mixture into the egg yolks, whisking constantly. Gradually add the yolk mixture back to the hot milk, whisking constantly. Continue to cook, stirring all the time, until the mixture reaches 82°C. Blend and pass through a sieve. Set in the fridge.

For The Burnt Chocolate Drops

Preheat the oven to 160°C.

Place the chocolate drops onto a tray lined with parchment paper, bake for 7 minutes.

For The Chocolate Shards

Melt both chocolate drops separately in a *bain-marie* or in the microwave, then pour onto a tray covered with parchment paper, mixing the two different types of chocolate. Set in the fridge.

For The Shortbread

Preheat the oven to 165°C.

Mix the butter and sugar until smooth, add the flour. Roll the dough in a cylindrical shape and put it in the fridge. Once set, cut the biscuits 1cm thick and bake for 8-10 minutes.

For The Chunky Cottage Cheese Cream

Mix the cottage cheese with the natural yoghurt.

To Assemble

Sprinkle the chocolate pot with cocoa powder and icing sugar. In a small cup, place a layer of chunky cottage cheese cream, followed by a layer of rhubarb compôte and the orange chocolate Anglaise. Add 1 burnt chocolate drop onto the cream and place a chocolate shard over the cup. Cover the shortbread with icing sugar, glaze it with a blow torch and break it in two. Place one half over the chocolate pot and the other on the plate.

Scatter popcorn and the remaining chocolate drops on the plates. Finish with a few dots of the cottage cheese cream and purée.

026
THE ADAMSON

127 South Street, St Andrews, Fife, KY16 9UH

01334 479 191
www.theadamson.com Twitter: @TheAdamson127
Facebook: The Adamson Instagram: theadamsonrestaurantbar

I n the heart of St Andrews at 127 South Street, The Adamson restaurant and cocktail bar is the perfect place to eat, drink and socialise. The venue continues to create a set of seasonal menus as part of the restaurant's dedication to using the freshest ingredients and commitment to sustainability with their suppliers.

The Adamson is a family business founded in 2012 by managing director Julie Lewis and occupies a historic site in the popular Scottish golf town. They lead the dynamic changes that are making St Andrews a 'must visit' destination for lovers of food and drink.

The stylish, vibrant and bustling restaurant and grill serves the best of Scotch beef, locally sourced seafood and produce from across Scotland's larder while the cocktail bar offers exquisite interiors with a bespoke and imaginative drinks menu.

This award-winning eatery consistently attracts diners from around the world who, when they find themselves in the home of golf, seek out The Adamson through choice.

"The Adamson has that desirable buzz you only get in restaurants that are highly successful: chefs working at full tilt and table after table of animated diners." Joanna Blythman, The Herald

SQUID, CHORIZO, BLACK OLIVE, BASIL

SERVES 2

🍷 *Terra de Asorei, Albariño, Rias Baixas
(Spain)*

Ingredients

Squid

1 baby squid tube (prepared, cleaned)
10g plain flour
table salt
10ml vegetable oil
5ml lemon juice

Black Olive Crumble

200g pitted black olives (drained)
5g cracked black pepper
15g lilliput capers
10g flat leaf parsley (finely chopped)
10g garlic (peeled, finely chopped)

Dried Cherry Tomatoes

10 cherry tomatoes (cut in half)
2g Maldon sea salt
2g cracked black pepper
10g garlic (chopped)
10g fresh thyme
20ml extra virgin olive oil

Chorizo

100g whole smoked chorizo
5ml balsamic vinegar
10ml extra virgin olive oil

Sauce

100ml red wine sauce
5ml extra virgin olive oil
30g tomatoes (*concasse*)

Garnish

micro basil

Method

For The The Squid

Cut the squid in half lengthways. Score inside diagonally with a sharp knife. Cut into 2½cm pieces, season with salt and plain flour.

To cook the squid, place the scored side down in a hot pan with a little vegetable oil. This will only take 30 seconds each side, so do this close to the time of plating and finish with the fresh lemon juice.

For The Black Olive Crumble (Prepare 2 days in advance)

Place all the ingredients in a blender and purée until a thick consistency has been reached. Spread the mixture onto a silicone mat and place in a dehydrator for 48 hours at 50°C, or in a low oven overnight. Once cold, blitz again in a blender until you have a crumble-like consistency. Set aside.

For The Dried Cherry Tomatoes (Prepare ahead)

Preheat the oven to 160°C (fan).

Gently combine all the ingredients in a bowl. Once fully incorporated, arrange the tomatoes cut-side up on a tray and cook in the oven for 8 minutes. While hot, place in a dehydrator for 6 hours. Alternatively, place in a low oven overnight.

For The Chorizo

Slice the chorizo using a meat slicer (1-2mm thickness). Make a vinaigrette using the balsamic and oil, brush the chorizo with the vinaigrette and leave somewhere warm to take on the flavour.

For The Sauce

Heat the red wine sauce. Once boiling, whisk in the olive oil until fully *emulsified*.

For the tomato *concasse*, score the plum tomatoes with a cross and remove the eye of the tomato with a turning knife. Place tomatoes in rapid boiling water until the skin blisters, then plunge into ice cold water for 5 minutes. Quarter the tomatoes lengthways and remove all the seeds. Cut the flesh into desired shape (squares/diamonds are most common).

To Serve

Serve as pictured, garnished with micro basil.

DUCK, SWEET POTATO, SPRING ONION, POPPY SEED, CHILLI, GINGER & CORIANDER

SERVES 2

 Fleurie La Madone, Beaujolais
(France)

Ingredients

Duck

1 x 140g duck breast
10ml vegetable oil
25g unsalted butter
1 sprig thyme
table salt (pinch of)

Sweet Potato

1 sweet potato (peeled)
100ml chicken stock
50g butter, salt and pepper

Poppy Seed Sheets

100g Red Rooster potatoes (peeled, cooked)
50g egg whites
25g poppy seeds
salt and pepper

Duck Skin Crumble

1 duck skin
10g Maldon sea salt
50g panko breadcrumbs

Carrot Purée

50g caster sugar, 50ml water
200g carrots (peeled, grated)
salt and pepper
10ml chicken or vegetable stock
100ml double cream

Sauce

50ml red wine sauce
10g red chillies (finely diced)
10g root ginger (peeled, finely diced)
10g coriander leaves
50g fresh sweetcorn kernels

Garnish

2 spring onions (sliced lengthways)
micro coriander

Method

For The Duck

Score the skin with a sharp knife across the whole breast in 1cm intervals. Place all the ingredients in a vacuum pack. Seal the duck tightly and cook at 56°C in a water bath for 1 hour. To finish, place the duck skin-side down in a medium heated pan with the vegetable oil and cook the skin until golden brown. Turn over and leave to rest. Alternatively, pan fry until the skin is crispy, then cook in the oven (180°C fan) for 10-15 minutes checking regularly.

For The Sweet Potato

Preheat the oven to 160°C (fan).

Cut the potato into 1cm slices and cut with a round cutter. Place the rounds of potato in a shallow tray with hot stock, butter and seasoning. Bake for 25-30 minutes until soft.

For The Poppy Seed Sheets

Mash the potato and mix with the egg white. Spread thinly on a silicone mat, dust with poppy seeds and dry out in a low oven.

For The Duck Skin Crumble

Preheat the oven to 150°C (fan).

Sprinkle the skin with salt and sandwich between 2 trays. Cook for 45 minutes. Once cool, blitz in a blender with the breadcrumbs to a crumble.

For The Carrot Purée

Combine the sugar and water in a wide, heavy-based pan to make a light caramel. Once golden, add the carrots and seasoning and cook for 10-15 minutes until the carrots are soft. Add the stock and reduce by half, add the cream, then reduce by half. Transfer to a Thermomix and blitz on high heat until a smooth consistency has been reached. Pass through a fine sieve. Place in a small squeezy bottle and leave in a warm place. Alternatively, blitz in a blender and pass through a fine sieve.

For The Sauce

Bring the red wine sauce to the boil. Stir in all the ingredients and serve immediately to retain freshness.

To Serve

Serve as pictured with the spring onions and micro coriander.

SALTED CARAMEL CREME BRULEE, BANANA, CHOCOLATE

SERVES 4

🍷 *Smokey Old Fashioned: Maker's Mark Bourbon,
Bitters, Maple, Syrup & Applewood Smoke*

Ingredients

Caramel Crème Brûlée

100g caster sugar
500ml double cream
5 egg yolks (100g)
Demerara sugar (to dust)

Salted Caramel Purée

1 tin condensed milk
2g Maldon sea salt

Aerated Chocolate

225g dark chocolate (53%)
45ml grapeseed oil

Cocoa Crumble

15g cocoa powder
50g plain flour
40g caster sugar
50g unsalted butter

Banana Crisps

100g bananas (peeled)
30g caster sugar
20g unsalted butter
10g plain flour

Popcorn

20g unsalted butter
20ml vegetable oil
40g popcorn kernels

Garnish

fudge pieces
micro coriander

metal rings (lined with cling film)
tray lined with greaseproof paper (frozen)

Method

For The Caramel Crème Brûlée (Prepare ahead)

Preheat the oven to 95°C (fan).

Make a light caramel with 50g of sugar in a wide, heavy-based pan. Once caramel, add the cream and reboil. In a separate bowl, whisk the yolks and remaining sugar. Pour the cream onto the egg mix, then pass through a fine sieve. Pour the mixture into the prepared rings and cook for 45-60 minutes. Refrigerate for 2-3 hours. To finish, dust with Demerara and caramelise with a blow torch.

For The Salted Caramel Purée

Cook the condensed milk in its tin for 3-4 hours in simmering water (do not allow to boil dry!). Once cold, add the sea salt, blitz in a blender, pass through a fine sieve and place in a squeezy bottle and keep somewhere warm.

For The Aerated Chocolate

Warm the chocolate and oil in a *bain-marie*. Take the chocolate to 45°C. Put the chocolate in an espuma gun and charge 3 times with gas. Spray onto the frozen tray and return to the freezer. Once frozen, break up into desired sizes. Alternatively, crumble a bar of 70% cocoa solids dark chocolate.

For The Cocoa Crumble

Preheat the oven to 160°C (fan).

Rub all the ingredients together, place on a tray and bake for about 30 minutes. Once cold, break up with a knife.

For The Banana Crisps

Preheat the oven to 150°C (fan).

Blitz all the ingredients in a blender. Spread out as thinly as possible on a large tray. Cook for 20-25 minutes until golden brown. Once cold, break into large pieces.

For The Popcorn

Add the ingredients to a pan, cover with the lid, then place a tray on top. Heat over a medium heat until the popcorn starts popping. When finished, take off the heat.

To Serve

Serve as pictured.

APPLECROSS INN

Shore Street, Applecross, Wester Ross, IV54 8LR

01520 744 262
www.applecross.uk.com/inn Twitter: @applecrossinn Facebook: @applecross.inn

The Applecross Inn remains a major tourist destination in Scotland and continues to attract visitors from all over the world. It appears in many publications and reviews as a must visit place.

The dining menus offer plenty of choice and with food served all day every day, it's always busy! Head chef Robert Macrae trained with the best in London before returning to his birthplace, attracted by the quality and freshness of the produce from the land, sea and shore. Creel-caught prawns (langoustines) and squat lobsters, crabs, hand-dived scallops and lobsters are delivered direct from the local fishing boat to the Inn. Fresh sustainable white fish arrives daily from both the east and the west coasts of Scotland. Scottish meats including local venison, beef and pork are also available.

For dessert why not try some of Aron's hand-made ice cream from Applecross Ices, produced exclusively for the Inn. He creates a wide range of winning flavours including golden syrup, bramble and apple, malt whisky and honey and Italian cherry. They are available from the Inn or from Applecross Inn-Side Out, the outdoor food truck, which also serves the Inn's famous fish and chips, hot/cold drinks and snacks.

The Inn has seven ensuite bedrooms and a lively, welcoming bar. The bar has a roaring fire on cold days and lovely shoreside outdoor seating for the warmer months, with spectacular views across the sea to the Isles of Raasay and Skye. The bar offers a great selection of drinks including ten Scottish gins, over 50 malt whiskies, a fantastic range of wines (all available by the glass) and local real ales. None more local than those now being produced by the newly formed Applecross Brewing Company. A dram for every occasion!

AppleCross Ices

APPLECROSS
Inn-Side Out

Handmade ...

APPLECROSS INN
welcomes you to

Applecross-Inn-Side-Out
FOR
Fresh Coffee, Tea,
Hot Chocolate, Cold Drinks

Freshly made Sandwiches
Our famous FISH & CHIPS

Aron's Handmade Ice Creams
(exclusive to the Inn)

Cakes, Chocolate, Crisps, Fruit.

Build your own Picnic!

Open 10-6pm & later in
good weather & busy times.

Judith Fish, the Inn's proprietor for the last 30 years and Good Pub Guide Landlady of the Year 2017, and her staff provide guests (many of whom are regulars) and customers with warm hospitable service, lovely freshly cooked meals and a great range of drinks.

WARM SALAD OF PIGEON BREAST, CRISPY BACON & PINE NUTS, CELERIAC REMOULADE

SERVES 4

Roccamora, Schola Sarmenti (Italy)
Explosive aromas of spice, leather and tobacco
with a fruity finish. This is a vigorous wine that
will tantalise your palate with its velvety
structure, softened by the light tannins that leave
a nice, lingering aftertaste.

Ingredients

Salad Dressing (Makes more than required)

6 tsp Dijon mustard
1 tsp wholegrain mustard
50g honey
500ml white wine vinegar
500ml olive oil
1 shallot (peeled, sliced)
2 cloves garlic
salt and pepper
1 lemon (juice of)

Celeriac Remoulade

½ small celeriac
1 tsp English mustard
1 tbsp mayonnaise
½ lemon (juice of)
salt and pepper

Pigeon

a little oil (to seal)
4 rashers bacon (finely sliced)
8 pigeon breasts
pine nuts (handful of)

To Serve

salad leaves

Method

For The Salad Dressing

Use an electric blender to whizz up all the ingredients together. Adjust seasoning to taste.

For The Celeriac Remoulade

Finely shred the celeriac, then fold in all the other ingredients. Keep chilled.

For The Pigeon

Preheat the oven to 240°C.

Heat the oil in an ovenproof pan, add the bacon, stir and cook for 1 minute.

Slice the breasts in half and add to the pan. Toss together to seal and colour. Place the pan in the oven for 2 minutes only. Remove from the oven, add 2 tablespoons of the salad dressing and the pine nuts. Lightly season and toss the pan to combine the ingredients.

Chef's Tip

These are locally sourced shot birds... so look out for shot! Do not overcook the pigeon.

To Serve

Serve on a plate dressed with salad leaves. Top with the celeriac remoulade.

KUNE KUNE PORK SAUSAGES, RICH ONION & ALE GRAVY, CREAMED MASHED POTATO, CARROT & SWEDE MASH

SERVES 4

 Applecross Brewing Company Sanctuary Ale from the newly opened Applecross Brewery.

Ingredients

Kune Kune Pork Sausages

1kg lean pork
250g pork fat
4 sage leaves
1 tsp allspice
black and white pepper (to season)
sea salt (generous sprinkling of)
chilled water (as required)
natural sausage skins (soaked for 2 hours)
rapeseed oil

Rich Onion And Ale Gravy

butter (knob of)
6 shallots (sliced)
6 mushrooms (sliced)
2 chicken wings
1 clove garlic (chopped)
1 sprig thyme (picked)
500ml real ale from Applecross Brewing Company
50ml port
150ml chicken stock
1 tsp redcurrant jelly
salt and pepper
3 medium onions (cut in half, sliced)

Carrot And Swede Mash

3 carrots (peeled, diced)
1 swede (peeled, diced)
salt and pepper
30g butter

Mashed Potato

4 portions hot mashed potato
3 tbsp apple purée
1 tbsp wholegrain mustard

mincer, sausage machine

Method

For The Kune Kune Pork Sausages

Combine the pork, pork fat and seasoning with enough water to achieve a dropping consistency. Pass the meat through the mincer twice. Fry off a small patty of the sausages to check the seasoning and adjust if necessary. Using a sausage machine, make the sausages allowing 3 per person.

Preheat the oven to 200°C.

Pan fry the sausages in a little rapeseed oil until well sealed. Transfer to the oven and cook for 10-12 minutes until golden brown.

Chef's Tip

You can make variations to the sausages by adding garlic, leek, onion, tomatoes and endless herbs and spices.

For The Rich Onion And Ale Gravy

Melt the butter in a frying pan. Over a medium heat, cook the shallots, mushrooms, chicken wings, half the garlic and half the thyme. Pour in the real ale and port and reduce to a syrup over a fairly high heat. Add the chicken stock and simmer for about 1 hour. Add the remaining thyme and garlic to the gravy, along with the redcurrant jelly.

Season and strain.

Meanwhile, caramelise the sliced onions until dark brown. Pour the gravy stock over the onions and simmer for 20 minutes.

For The Carrot And Swede Mash

Cook the carrots and swede in boiling, salted water until soft. Mash, season, then stir in the butter.

For The Mashed Potato

Combine the elements and keep warm.

To Assemble

Spoon a portion of mashed potato onto each plate. Place the sausages on top, then pour over some onion gravy. Serve with the carrot and swede mash on one side.

STICKY TOFFEE PUDDING, BUTTERSCOTCH SAUCE

SERVES 4

Glen Garioch 12-Year-Old Malt Whisky
With its dark caramel nose, the whisky
complements this pudding very well.

Ingredients

Butterscotch Sauce

250g butter
150g caster sugar
80g dark brown sugar
280ml double cream

Sticky Toffee Pudding

2 tsp bicarbonate of soda
600ml boiling water
350g dates (chopped)
100g butter (softened)
160g caster sugar
160g dark brown sugar
4 eggs
350g self-raising flour (sieved)

To Serve

Italian vanilla ice cream

25cm baking tray (lined with parchment)

Method

For The Butterscotch Sauce

Melt the butter, add the sugars and stir until dissolved. Pour in the double cream and bring to the boil. Set aside.

For The Sticky Toffee Pudding

Coat the bottom of the baking tray with a layer of butterscotch sauce and place in the freezer until needed.

Preheat the oven to 180ºC.

Add the boiling water and bicarbonate of soda to the dates and leave to soak for 25 minutes.

Cream the butter with both the sugars, slowly add the eggs then mix in the flour until well combined. Carefully, as it will splash, stir in the soaked dates with all the liquid. Transfer the mixture to the baking tray and bake in the oven for 1 hour, turning after 30 minutes. When cooked, make small holes over the cake surface and pour over a little more butterscotch sauce whilst it is still hot.

To Assemble

Serve as pictured with the Italian vanilla ice cream.

Chef's Tip

You can't have too much sauce on this pudding - we think it's the reason we receive such good reviews for the recipe!

046
BOROUGH

50-54 Henderson Street, Leith, Edinburgh, EH6 6DE

Tel: 0131 629 2525
www.boroughrestaurant.com Twitter: @Borough_Leith Facebook: BoroughLeith

The latest addition to Leith's food scene, Borough is comfortably woven into the neighbourhood with a modern menu of seasonal cuisine.

The restaurant is a new chapter for head chef Darren Murray. Previously head chef at Norn and with years of Michelin starred experience, Darren is turning the page with his seasonal, contemporary menu.

Standing on the corner of Henderson Street in the heart of Leith, the space is bright and welcoming, inviting guests in for lunch and dinner, Wednesday through Sunday.

Designed with flexibility in mind, Borough's considered menu draws on sustainable produce cooked with flair for a thoroughly modern dining experience. Darren is joined by respected restaurant manager Richard Kyle, who is a well-known industry figure in the Edinburgh hospitality scene.

Darren's cooking is precise, bold and focuses on using the best seasonal ingredients in simple forms, all of which has become a signature element of his own cooking.

With an evolving menu, linked to season and quality, that has an 'à la carte' focus, Borough is set to delight its customers; Leith locals and visitors alike.

LEITH

Borough

50-54 HENDERSON ST

Comfortably woven into the neighbourhood, Borough serves up modern, seasonal dishes alongside carefully sourced wines in the heart of Leith.

MACKEREL, GREEN STRAWBERRY, ELDERFLOWER

SERVES 4

 Weingut Eichinger, Grüner Veltliner Wechselberg, 2016 (Austria)

Ingredients

4 mackerel fillets
salt (to season)

Pickle Liquor

10ml vinegar
20g sugar
30ml water
10g elderflower

To Finish And Serve

50g radish (diced)
100g green strawberries (sliced)
5g elderflower

Method

For The Pickle Liquor

Bring all the ingredients to a fast boil, then chill.

For The Mackerel

Dice the mackerel, dress with the pickle *liquor* and season with salt.

To Finish And Serve

Mix the diced radish into the mackerel and place a heaped tablespoon onto each plate. Top neatly with the sliced strawberries and sprinkle the elderflowers on top.

Chef's Tip

Make sure all ingredients are the same temperature for the best results.

MUSSEL TAGLIATELLE, DILL, GHERKIN

SERVES 4

🍷 *Fallen Brewing, Odyssey Blonde (Scotland)*

Method

For The Tagliatelle

Whisk the eggs and yolks together. Make a well with the flour and slowly add the eggs to the middle, mixing together with a fork. When it resembles a broken dough, start kneading until smooth, about 5-10 minutes. Rest for 1 hour. Roll out with a pasta machine and cut to tagliatelle. Fresh shop bought tagliatelle works well here also.

For The Mussels

Wash and scrub the mussels. Bring a pan to the heat, add the mussels and quickly pour in the wine. Cover with a lid for 2 minutes until they start to open. Remove half from the shell and blend on a high heat whilst warm with the olive oil and butter.

To Serve

Cook the tagliatelle in salted, boiling water, drain, then return to the pan. Mix in the mussel cream and the whole mussels. Add to bowls and top with the dill and diced gherkin.

Chef's Tip

Cook the pasta in the mussel sauce for 2 minutes to achieve a better consistency to the dish.

Ingredients

Tagliatelle

3 whole large eggs
2 large egg yolks
500g '00' flour

Mussels

1kg mussels
100ml white wine
150ml extra virgin olive oil
50g butter

Garnish

20g dill gherkins (diced)
10g dill fronds (picked)

GOOSEBERRY, BAY LEAF, MERINGUE

SERVES 6-8

Cantina Bassoli, Lambrusco Grasparossa Ciacaron, Red (Italy)

Ingredients

750g green gooseberries

Meringue
100g egg white
200g caster sugar

Bay Ice Cream
500ml whole milk
500ml double cream
50g bay leaves
200g caster sugar
210g egg yolk

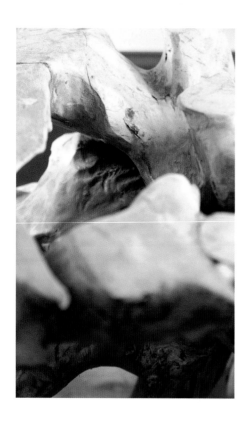

Method

For The Meringue

Preheat the oven to 60°C (fan).

Whisk the egg white with a third of the sugar. When tripled in volume, slowly add the rest of the sugar. Spread thinly on greaseproof paper and bake for 2 hours until dry.

For The Bay Ice Cream

Bring the milk, cream and bay leaves to a slow simmer. Meanwhile, mix the sugar and egg yolks together. When ready, pour the hot cream slowly over the egg mixture, constantly whisking. Place back on the heat and slowly cook until the mixture coats the back of a spoon. Chill the mixture, then pass through a sieve. Churn in an ice cream machine.

Chef's Tip

Dry leftover bay leaves at your lowest oven temperature, then blitz to a fine powder for added flavour when put into sauces or sprinkled on top of chocolate.

For The Gooseberries

Cook 500g of the gooseberries until jam consistency, then chill. Slice the rest of the gooseberries and reserve.

To Assemble

Spoon the gooseberry jam on the bottom of each plate and add the sliced gooseberries. Place a large scoop of ice cream on top and cover with shards of the meringue, dusted with bay leaf powder.

056
CAIL BRUICH

725 Great Western Road, Glasgow, G12 8QX

0141 334 6265
www.cailbruich.co.uk Twitter: @CailBruich Facebook: Cail Bruich

Located in the heart of Glasgow's vibrant West End - adjacent to Glasgow Botanic Gardens and around the corner from bustling Byres Road and Ashton Lane - Cail Bruich celebrated its 10th anniversary in business during 2018.

Owned and run by the Charalambous family, this stylish restaurant and bar offers casual, modern Scottish dining and select drinks. Cail Bruich is widely-regarded, by both public and peers alike, as one of the finest restaurants and bars in Scotland's most populous city, where a quality hospitality sector thrives.

Photograph by Keith Gooderham, Greenshoots Photography

Awarded with 3 AA Rosettes, the kitchen brigade - under the leadership of Chris Charalambous - passionately crafts menus with an appreciation for the freshest, seasonal ingredients and produce harvested from Scotland's outstanding natural larder. The restaurant also boasts its own organic kitchen garden at the rear of the building, where a variety of vegetables, herbs and soft fruits are nurtured, cultivated and hand-picked within a few feet of Cail Bruich's open kitchen.

Offering a number of flexible dining options; from relaxed multiple course tasting menus with carefully-curated wine pairings to prompt 2 course market menu lunches; Cail Bruich presents the choice of indulgent dining experiences and accessible, quality-focused meals to their guests. Open daily.

Photograph by Keith Gooderham, Greenshoots Photography

Cail Bruich offers contemporary Scottish cuisine, along with an eclectic selection of wines and spirits, in a stylish restaurant and bar conveniently located in the heart of Glasgow's West End.

MARINATED SCALLOP, BROWN CRAB, RHUBARB & ELDERFLOWER

SERVES 4

Peter Jakob Kühn Oestrich Lenchen Riesling
Kabinett - Rheingau 2016 (Germany)

Ingredients

Scallop Ceviche

8 extra large hand-dived scallops (*shucked*)
Maldon salt

Rhubarb And Elderflower Dressing

270g rhubarb (juiced)
30g tomato purée
100ml elderflower vinegar
100ml reduced shellfish bisque (reduced from 500ml shellfish stock. If unavailable, use tinned lobster bisque)
270ml extra virgin olive oil
5g salt
5g sugar
Ultratex (to thicken, optional)
chives, chervil, dill (handful of, chopped)
pickled elderflower heads (optional)

Pickled Rhubarb

100ml rhubarb vinegar
100ml elderflower vinegar
200g sugar
1kg rhubarb (topped, tailed)

Brown Crab Emulsion

80g pasteurised egg yolk
15g Dijon mustard
240g brown crab meat (passed through a sieve)
10g salt
40ml lemon juice
80g dried brioche breadcrumbs
360g roasted crab oil

Sea Herbs

50g samphire
25g sea purslane

Method

For The Scallop Ceviche

Remove the skirt and roe from the scallops. Wash and pat dry. Marinate the scallops in the rhubarb and elderflower dressing and serve raw.

> **Chef's Tip**
>
> Always buy hand-dived scallops in the shell. They are firmer, sweeter and much better for our environment.

For The Rhubarb And Elderflower Dressing

Blend all the ingredients, apart from the herbs, together until *emulsified* and thickened slightly. Add herbs just before serving.

For The Pickled Rhubarb

Simmer the vinegars and sugar together for 1 minute to make a light syrup. Place the rhubarb in a vacuum bag with the syrup and seal. Cook in a water bath set at 62°C for 8 minutes. It should still have a little crunch. Alternatively, place the rhubarb in a plastic container and pour the boiling syrup over. Remove once cooled.

For The Brown Crab Emulsion

Add the egg yolk, mustard, crab meat, salt, lemon juice and breadcrumbs to a blender. Blend on high for a few minutes until smooth, then reduce the speed to medium and slowly drizzle in the oil to make a thick mayonnaise. Adjust the seasoning if necessary and transfer to a piping bag.

For The Sea Herbs

Blanch the herbs in boiling water for 15 seconds, then refresh immediately in iced water. Dry on kitchen paper until ready to serve.

To Assemble The Dish

Slice the scallops horizontally, season with sea salt and lay on a plate. Pipe the crab *emulsion* over and around. Slice the rhubarb into 2cm slices and arrange over the scallops. Spoon the dressing over and finish with the sea herbs.

INVERURIE LAMB, VIOLET ARTICHOKE, ASPARAGUS, PEAS, GOAT'S CURD

SERVES 4

R López de Heredia Viña Tondonia Reserva - DOCa Rioja - 2004 (Spain)

Ingredients

Lamb Loin

1 short saddle of lamb (boned, trimmed of all fat and sinew)
50g lamb fat
1 sprig thyme
2 bay leaves

Sweetbreads

1kg lamb sweetbreads (trimmed)
50g lamb fat
1 sprig thyme
1 bay leaf
seasoned flour

Violet Artichokes

4 large violet artichokes (peeled, trimmed)
105ml rapeseed oil
35ml apple cider vinegar
5g fennel seeds
2g lemon zest
1 sprig thyme
10g salt

Asparagus

8 large green asparagus spears (trimmed)

Pea Purée

500g frozen peas
250g spinach

Garden Peas

250g fresh pea pods

To Finish And Serve

oil (to seal)
butter (knob of)
100g fresh goat's curd
100ml lamb jus

Method

For The Lamb Loin

Cut the lamb saddle into 2 loins, roughly 300g each. Vac pack the loins with the fat and herbs. Cook in a water bath at 54°C for 20 minutes. Leave to rest. Alternatively, seal in a hot pan until golden. Reduce the heat, then add 50g butter, 1 bay leaf and 1 sprig of thyme and baste with the foaming butter. Place in a hot oven for 2 minutes, then remove from the pan and rest.

For The Sweetbreads

Vac pack the sweetbreads with the fat and herbs. Cook at 64°C for 45 minutes, then chill immediately. Drain and pat dry. Set aside. Alternatively, pan fry.

For The Violet Artichokes

Vac pack the artichoke hearts and stalks with all the ingredients and cook at 85°C for 45 minutes until tender. Refresh in iced water, then remove from the bag and strain the vinaigrette. Reserve both separately. Alternatively, gently poach until tender.

For The Asparagus

Blanch the asparagus in heavily salted water for 1-2 minutes, refresh immediately in iced water. Trim off the tips, then slice the stalk into 2cm rounds.

For The Pea Purée

Blanch the vegetables for 2 minutes in heavily salted water. Refresh immediately in iced water. Blend with a little cooking water until smooth. Pass through a *chinois*. Season.

For The Garden Peas

Blanch for 1 minute in boiling salted water. Refresh immediately in iced water. Discard the outer skin so all that remains is the inner green pea flesh.

To Assemble The Dish

Seal the loins in a little oil over a high heat until browned all over. Reduce the heat and add butter. When foaming, baste the lamb for 1 minute. Rest for 5 minutes.

Lightly dust the sweetbreads in seasoned flour. Seal in oil over a medium heat until crisp and brown all over. Reduce the heat, add a knob of butter and, when foaming, baste the sweetbreads until golden. Drain on kitchen paper. Warm the artichoke, peas and asparagus in a little *emulsion* (50:50 butter/water). Drain on kitchen paper. Swirl the warm pea purée on a plate. Serve as pictured finishing with a few drops of goat's curd and *jus*.

Chef's Tip

Make sure the lamb is properly rested before carving or it will be dry. This is a very seasonal dish and should only be prepared in the height of summer when the produce is at its peak.

SHEEP'S YOGHURT PARFAIT, PERTHSHIRE STRAWBERRY, FENNEL POLLEN, TARRAGON

SERVES 8

Sepp Moser Pinot Blanc, Beerenauslese, 2012
(Austria)

Ingredients

Sheep's Yoghurt Parfait

135g egg yolks
90ml water
85g sugar
35g fondant
50ml cream
2 leaves gelatine (soaked in cold water)
400g sheep's yoghurt
100g cocoa butter
100g white chocolate

Fennel Pollen Meringue

100g egg white
200g caster sugar
1g fennel pollen

Tarragon Oil

100g tarragon (*blanched*, refreshed in iced water, squeezed dry)
200ml pomace oil

Strawberries

500g strawberries
100ml stock syrup
10g tarragon leaves

To Serve

10g tarragon leaves (picked)
10g sweet cicely leaves (picked, optional)

8 savarin moulds

Method

For The Sheep's Yoghurt Parfait (Prepare ahead)

Place the egg yolks in a stand mixer with the whisk attachment.

Combine the water, sugar and fondant in a heavy-based pan and bring slowly to the boil. Cook until the temperature reaches 116°C. Once this happens, start whisking the yolks. Continue cooking the syrup until it reaches 121°C. Remove from the heat, let it stand for 1 minute, then slowly stream the hot syrup over the whisking yolks. Continue whipping until cool.

Warm the cream slightly, then stir in the gelatine, add this to the egg yolks. Fold in the sheep's yoghurt, then place the mix in savarin moulds to set in the freezer overnight. Once set, melt the cocoa butter and white chocolate together, then place in a paint gun. Spray the frozen parfait with this mix until coated. Freeze until set. Alternatively, paint the parfaits with the chocolate mix.

For The Fennel Pollen Meringue (Prepare ahead)

Make a French meringue by whisking the egg white and adding the sugar in 4 stages. Spread on a mat and dust with fennel pollen. Dehydrate in a low oven overnight until crisp.

For The Tarragon Oil

Blend the oil and tarragon in a Thermomix at 60°C for 8 minutes. *Macerate* for 1 hour, then strain through muslin. Keep at room temperature until required. Alternatively, blend with a hand blender. Leave to sit for 1 hour, then strain.

For The Strawberries

Heat the stock syrup with the tarragon leaves. Leave to cool, then strain. Cut the strawberries into halves or quarters and dress with the tarragon syrup.

To Assemble The Dish

Lay the parfait on a chilled plate. Arrange the strawberries around and on top with the herbs and meringue. Finally, pour the tarragon oil onto the top of the parfait.

Chef's Tip

Simplicity is the key to this dessert. Make sure all elements are prepared correctly and you're on to a winner! Scottish strawberries are a must!

066
CASTLE TERRACE

33/35 Castle Terrace, Edinburgh , EH1 2EL

0131 229 1222
www.castleterracerestaurant.com Twitter: @dominicjack Facebook: dominicjack
Instagram: castle_terrace_restaurant

Castle Terrace Restaurant opened its doors in July 2010, introducing a new dining experience to the city of Edinburgh. Combining the culinary expertise and flair of the team behind award-winning Michelin star restaurant The Kitchin, Castle Terrace Restaurant is led by Edinburgh-born Dominic Jack. Nestled underneath Edinburgh Castle, the stylish award-winning restaurant offers a truly unique fine dining experience with a menu created from chef patron Dominic Jack's innovative cooking skills.

Castle Terrace presents modern British cuisine influenced by learned French cooking techniques and an appreciation of the best ingredients available from Scotland's outstanding natural larder. The well-balanced and exciting menu reflects Dominic's many years of training in some of Europe's top Michelin star kitchens - such as l'Arpège, restaurant Les Elysées and Taillevent in Paris, where he spent many years working with Michelin 3-star chef Alain Solivérès.

The restaurant's philosophy - 'From Nature to Plate' - is a true representation of the finest and freshest seasonal Scottish ingredients and offers elegant and wonderfully balanced dishes, all prepared with a delicate flair and passion.

'From Nature to Plate'

CHICKEN LIVER PARFAIT, GRAPE

SERVES 4

 Muscat 'Tamianka', Terra Tangra, Thracian Valley, 2017 (Bulgaria)

Ingredients

Chicken Liver Parfait

2 shallots (diced)
120ml cognac
120ml port
62g duck fat
62g unsalted butter
225g fresh chicken livers
4 egg yolks
225ml double cream
salt and pepper

Grape Jelly

2 litres grape juice
1 tbsp kappa carrageenan

Rosemary And Garlic Grissini

200g *clarified butter*
10 cloves garlic
3 sprigs rosemary
62g butter
5g yeast
1 tsp olive oil
62ml water
2½g sugar
6g salt
250g flour
green fat-soluble food colouring (as required)
red fat-soluble food colouring (as required)

demi-sphere moulds
loaf tin

Method

For The Chicken Liver Parfait (Prepare ahead)

Cover the shallots in the port and cognac, then reduce over a medium heat until dry.

Melt the duck fat and butter together.

Combine the livers, yolks, cream, melted fats and shallots in a food processor and blend until smooth.

Pass through a fine sieve and season with salt and fine pepper.

Cook in a loaf tin inside another tray with water *(bain-marie)* at 90°C until the internal temperature reaches 62°C.

Once cool, pipe into small demi-sphere moulds and freeze.

For The Grape Jelly

Reduce 1 litre of the grape juice by half. Add the remaining litre and the kappa carrageenan and bring to a rapid boil. Remove from the heat and cool down to approximately 40°C.

Using a toothpick, dip the frozen parfait into the jelly until nicely coated. Leave in the fridge to defrost.

Chef's Tip

Dip 3 parfait at a time so they stay frozen when dipping.

For The Rosemary And Garlic Grissini

Melt the *clarified butter* with the garlic and rosemary, leave to infuse.

In a small pot, combine the butter, yeast, olive oil, water, sugar, salt and warm until 26°C. Put the flour in a large pot and make a well in the middle, add the yeast mixture and knead until combined.

Place in the fridge for 1 hour to firm up.

Preheat the oven to 180°C (fan).

Roll out the grissini until approximately 3mm thickness. Using a leaf cutter or stencil, cut the grissini. Halve the *clarified butter* and mix each half with the food colourings. Paint the leaves with the coloured butters and bake for 7 minutes or until crisp.

To Serve

Serve as pictured.

ROASTED RED LEGGED PARTRIDGE, AUTUMNAL VEGETABLES

SERVES 4

 Etna Rosso, Tenuta Delle Terre Nere, Sicilia, 2016 (Italy)

Ingredients

Braised Red Cabbage

¼ red cabbage (finely sliced)
240ml red wine
1 stick cinnamon
2 tbsp brown sugar
salt (pinch of)

Roasted Partridge And Vegetables

1 potato
¼ celeriac
¼ turnip
1 stick salsify
1 carrot
1 apple
olive oil (drizzle of)
salt (pinch of)
2 oven-ready red legged partridge

Crispy Partridge Leg

1 carrot (roughly chopped)
1 stick celery (roughly chopped)
½ white onion (roughly chopped)
500ml chicken stock
120ml veal stock
4 partridge legs
100g flour
2 egg yolks
1 tbsp double cream
100g breadcrumbs
oil (to deep fry)

Garnish

10 red grapes (sliced)
1 apple (cut into batons)

Method

For The Braised Red Cabbage

Place the sliced cabbage in a pot with the red wine, cinnamon and sugar. Gently cook down until the cabbage is soft, adding more red wine if needed. Season with salt and more sugar if necessary.

For The Roasted Partridge And Vegetables

Preheat the oven to 200°C (fan).

Peel the vegetables and apple, then cut into desired shapes. Toss with olive oil and salt, then place in the bottom of a roasting tray. Place the partridge on top and roast for approximately 20 minutes. Remove from the oven and let rest for 5 minutes.

Strain off the cooking liquids and reduce to a sauce consistency.

For The Crispy Partridge Leg

Cook the vegetables until golden in a medium-sized pot. Add the stocks and bring to a gentle simmer. Add the partridge legs and cook for 30 minutes or until the meat is falling from the bone. Clean the bones, removing all sinew. Strain the meat and vegetables from the stock through a fine sieve, then reduce the stock to a sauce-like consistency.

Pick the meat from the legs, then mix with the reduced stock and leave to cool. Once cool, divide the mixture into 4 even-sized balls. Toss the balls through the flour, shaking off any excess. Beat together the yolks and cream, pass the balls through the egg mix, then toss the balls through the breadcrumbs and insert a cleaned bone. Deep fry (180°C) in oil until crispy, 3-5 minutes.

To Serve

Carve the breast from the partridge, then glaze with the reduced cooking liquid. Garnish with sliced grapes, apple batons, braised red cabbage and the roasted vegetables.

HAZELNUT PRALINE ECLAIR, CHOCOLATE BROWNIE

SERVES 4

Primitivo di Manduria, Tenuta Giuseppe Attanasio, Puglia, 2011 (Italy)

Ingredients

Eclair

250ml whole milk
100g butter (diced)
130g flour (sifted)
4 medium eggs
salt (pinch of)

Chocolate Brownie

2 medium eggs
75g dark brown sugar
75g caster sugar
150g butter
90g dark chocolate (70%)
75g plain flour
8g cocoa powder
100g white chocolate buttons

Hazelnut Praline Mousse

100g hazelnut praline
225g milk chocolate buttons
125ml whipping cream
50g granulated sugar
3 egg yolks
125ml double cream (whipped)

Crème Chantilly

100ml whipping cream
1 tbsp icing sugar
1 tsp vanilla paste

Garnish (Optional)

cocoa powder
chocolate sauce

30cm x 20cm oven tray (greased, lined)

Method

For The Eclair

Preheat the oven to 180°C (fan).

Bring the milk and butter to a gentle simmer in a medium-sized pot. Remove from the heat and add in the flour, beating until smooth. Place back on a low heat and stir for 4 more minutes, the mixture should come away from the sides. Remove from the heat and leave to cool for 5 minutes. Add 1 egg to the mixture at a time, making sure you have completely mixed in each egg before you add the next. You should have a stiff, glossy choux pastry. Place the choux into a piping bag with a ½cm nozzle. Pipe 10cm lines of pastry onto a silicone mat and bake in the oven for 10 minutes. Leave to cool.

For The Chocolate Brownie

Preheat the oven to 180°C (fan).

Beat the eggs and sugars in a Kitchen Aid until doubled in volume.

Melt the butter and dark chocolate together.

At a slow speed, pour the chocolate mix over the egg mixture whilst continuing to beat. Stir in the flour and cocoa powder and mix until combined. Fold through the white chocolate buttons. Pour into the prepared tray and bake for 15 minutes. Leave to cool.

For The Hazelnut Praline Mousse

Melt the hazelnut praline, chocolate buttons and whipping cream together in a small pot.

In a separate pot, bring the sugar to a caramel.

Carefully add the praline and cream mixture into the caramel, mix until smooth. While still warm, quickly beat in the egg yolks, then leave to cool. When cool, fold through the whipped cream and transfer to a piping back with a star nozzle.

> **Chef's Tip**
> Make the praline mousse a day in advance to allow it to set.

For The Crème Chantilly

Whip the cream, icing sugar and vanilla together to soft peaks.

To Assemble

Cut 10cm by 1cm strips of the brownie. Cut the éclairs in half. Place the bottom half on top of the brownie. Pipe the hazelnut praline mousse on top of the base, then the Crème Chantilly on top of that. Place the top of the éclair on and serve immediately. Garnish with cocoa powder and chocolate sauce, if desired.

076
CRAIG MILLAR @ 16 WEST END

16 West End, Anstruther, KY10 2BX

01333 730 327
www.16westend.com Twitter: @craigcmillar

Born and educated in Dundee, Craig Millar started his career with Crest Hotels in Buckinghamshire before moving back north of the border, working in several restaurants and hotels. Among them was Murrayshall House Hotel, under the guidance of Bruce Sangster. In 1998 Craig joined up with Tim Butler for what was to be a 13-year partnership at The Seafood Restaurant in St Monans and they went on to open The Seafood Restaurant, St Andrews, in 2003. It was during this period that the pair won accolades such as SLTN Restaurant of the Year, AA Restaurant of the Year, AA Wine List of the Year, AA Seafood Restaurant of the Year, CIS Restaurant of the Year, Scottish Restaurant Awards 'Speciality Restaurant of the Year'.

Both restaurants were also named 'Newcomer of the Year' in the Good Food Guide. Craig was also named 'Seafood Restaurant Chef of the Year' and he won 'Taste of Scotland Lamb Challenge'.

After a major renovation in June 2011, Craig took sole ownership of the St Monans Restaurant, renaming it Craig Millar @ 16 West End.

Within the first eight months, the restaurant picked up CIS Newcomer of the Year. The menu now includes more meat and game dishes, rather than just specialising in seafood, and Craig champions the use of local produce.

The restaurant occupies an old fisherman's cottage and features an 800-year-old freshwater well with mythical, healing powers. There is an open fire in the Victorian style lounge where pre-dinner or after-dinner drinks can be enjoyed and an outside terrace to use during the warmer weather. Picture windows in the restaurant's modern extension allow diners to admire views of the harbour.

The restaurant currently holds 2 AA Rosettes, is listed in The Good Food Guide, winner of Newcomer of the Year 2012 CIS Excellence Awards and finalist Restaurant of the Year 2014 CIS Excellence Awards.

WEST SHORE

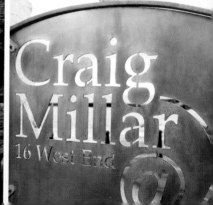

Craig Millar
16 West End

JERUSALEM ARTICHOKE PANNA COTTA

SERVES 4

🍷 *Grenache 'Old Bush Vine' Yalumba Barossa (Australia)*

Ingredients

Jerusalem Artichoke Panna Cotta

250g Jerusalem artichokes (peeled)
75g butter
rapeseed oil (splash of)
250ml whole milk
250ml whipping cream
salt
white pepper
3 sheets gelatine (soaked in cold water)

Garnish

white onion purée
pickled shimeji mushrooms
pickled shallot rings
micro mizuna

4 dariole moulds

Method

For The Jerusalem Artichoke Panna Cotta

Finely slice the artichokes.

Melt the butter in a pan with a splash of oil, add the sliced artichokes and sweat off until soft, trying not to colour them.

Add the milk and reduce by half, then add the cream and reduce by half. Remove from the heat and purée in a food processor until smooth.

Pass through a fine sieve and season to taste with the salt and white pepper.

Remove the gelatine from the cold water and add to the purée while still warm. Pour the mixture into the moulds and allow to set in the fridge for 2-3 hours, or ideally overnight.

To Serve

Once set, demould by briefly dipping the moulds in hot water.

Place into a serving bowl, garnishing with onion purée, pickled mushrooms, shallot rings and mizuna leaves.

Chef's Tip

Add a little texture to the dish by deep frying thin slices of artichoke.

TOMATO & SHALLOT CRUSTED COD, SCALLOP, SPLIT HERB SAUCE, SEA VEGETABLES

SERVES 4

 Saskia, Chenin Blanc/Viognier, Miles Mossop, 2014, (Coastal Region, South Africa)

Ingredients

Herb Oil

100g chives
100g flat leaf parsley
200ml rapeseed oil

Herb Sauce

2 carrots (roughly chopped)
1 onion (diced)
2 sticks celery (roughly chopped)
1 bulb fennel (roughly chopped)
1 leek (sliced)
100g button mushrooms (sliced)
rapeseed oil (drizzle of)
500ml chicken stock
2 bay leaves
500ml fish stock
250ml whipping cream

Shallot Crust

50g butter
10ml rapeseed oil
1 shallot (finely diced)
100g panko breadcrumbs
50g dehydrated tomatoes (ground to a powder)
1 tbsp finely chopped chives
seasoning

Fish

4 x 150g pieces cod fillet
4 large hand-dived scallops (white meat only)
butter (knob of)
8 stalks wild sea kale (halved)
30g samphire

Method

For The Herb Oil

Place the chives and parsley into a food processor and slowly add the oil whilst the machine is running on high. Strain through a muslin cloth.

For The Herb Sauce

Sweat off the vegetables in a little oil without browning them. Add the chicken stock and bay leaves and reduce by half. Pour in the fish stock and reduce again. Add the cream, reduce by half, then strain through a fine sieve.

For The Shallot Crust

Melt half the butter with the oil in a pan and sweat off the diced shallot, colouring slightly. Add the breadcrumbs with the rest of the butter and all other ingredients. Season, then spread out onto a tray.

> **Chef's Tip**
>
> If you can't dehydrate tomatoes, you can use powdered tomato soup instead.

To Cook The Fish And Serve

Heat up a non-stick frying pan with a little oil, season the cod and place skin-side down in the pan along with the scallops. When slightly coloured, flip over, spoon some of the crumb onto the cod and place under a hot grill until cooked (the scallops will be ready before the cod). Meanwhile, heat up a small sauté pan and add a little knob of butter and a splash of oil. Throw in the kale and samphire with a little splash of water (this will take less than a minute).

Place the cod and a scallop onto a plate and garnish with the sea vegetables. Warm the sauce, add some of the herb oil, mix and pour onto the plate.

CHOCOLATE CREMEUX

SERVES 12

Pedro Ximénez, Don Guido, 20-Year-Old, Williams
& Humbert, Jerez (Spain)

Ingredients

Base

125g Bourbon biscuits (blitzed)
60g butter (melted)
125g Cara Crackine

Crémeux

45g egg yolks
23g caster sugar
55ml whole milk
125ml double cream
½ vanilla pod (scraped)
1 sheet gelatine (softened in cold water)
125g dark chocolate (53%)
13g butter

Malt Ice Cream

3 egg yolks
130g caster sugar
500ml whole milk
150ml double cream
50g malt extract

Aerated Chocolate

300g dark chocolate
2 tbsp grapeseed oil

Salted Caramel

150ml double cream
150g sugar
40g butter
½ tsp sea salt

Chocolate Soil

65g ground almonds
65g sugar
35g plain flour
25g cocoa powder
30g butter (melted)

Garnish

micro mint leaves
meringue shards (optional)
tempered chocolate (optional)

Method

For The Base (Prepare ahead)
Combine the biscuits and butter. Line a tray with a double layer of cling film and spread out the biscuit evenly in the tray. Refrigerate. Roll out the Cara Crakine between 2 sheets of greaseproof paper and freeze for 30 minutes. Cut to the size of the tray and place on top of the biscuit. Set in the fridge until needed.

For The Crémeux (Prepare ahead)
Whisk the egg yolks and sugar in a mixer until fluffy.
Bring the milk, cream and vanilla to the boil, then stir in the gelatine.
Pour the cream mix into the egg yolks and mix slowly. Add the chocolate and butter and continue to whisk until fully melted.
Pour the mix on top of the biscuit base. Tap the tray a few times to remove any air bubbles. Set in the fridge overnight.

For The Malt Ice Cream (Prepare ahead)
Whisk together the egg yolks and sugar until light and fluffy.
Bring the milk to the boil and whisk into the egg yolks. Add the cream and return the mix to the pan, slowly heat until it coats the back of a spoon.
Stir in the malt extract until dissolved.
Place into a Paco Jet canister, leave to cool, then freeze for 24 hours. Alternatively, churn in an ice cream machine.

For The Aerated Chocolate
Melt the chocolate over a *bain-marie*. Mix in the oil and place in an espuma gun.
Add 3 charges and place the mix on a tray lined with cling film in the freezer to set quickly. If you haven't got an espuma gun buy a Wispa bar and chop it up!

For The Salted Caramel
Bring the cream to the boil and set aside.
Caramelise the sugar in a pan to a light golden brown colour. Remove from the heat. Slowly add the cream in small amounts whisking all the time. Once incorporated, add the butter, a little at a time, until each part has melted into the mix. Finally, add the salt and stir well. Leave to cool.

For The Chocolate Soil
Preheat the oven to 165ºC.
Combine all the ingredients well. Place on a tray lined with greaseproof paper and bake for 10 minutes or until dry and crisp.

To Finish
Cut the set crémeux into portions and place on plates. Use a blow torch over the top to give it a shine.
Break up the aerated chocolate and place 3 pieces on top. Put the salted caramel and chocolate soil to the side of the crémeux and *quenelle* a scoop of ice cream on top. Finish with micro mint leaves.

086
DALHOUSIE CASTLE

Bonnyrigg, Edinburgh, Midlothian, EH19 3JB

01875 820 153
www.dalhousiecastle.co.uk Twitter: @dalhousiecastle Instagram: dalhousie__castle

Dalhousie Castle's 'Dungeon Restaurant' is perhaps one of the most popular gastronomic venues in Scotland, and certainly one of the most unique. This enchanting castle boasts a 700 year history, and is Scotland's oldest inhabited castle. Its incredible guest list pays homage to its colourful past, including King Edward I, Sir Walter Scott, Oliver Cromwell and Queen Victoria.

Head chef Francois Giraud's modern European style is combined with Scottish influences to produce 2 AA Rosette cuisine which will excite and tantalise the palate. Francois sources the finest, freshest, local ingredients, heavily influenced by seasonality and availability.

Indeed, he works closely with a local butcher, who is supplied by a trusted network of farmers, where animal welfare, as well as quality, is taken into account when sourcing their meats, whether it be the most succulent Scottish grass-fed beef, free-range pork or wild venison.

Suits of armour and medieval paraphernalia are boldly displayed within the Dungeon, which has a surprisingly warm and welcoming ambience. Lit by candlelight, one cannot help but be enchanted by this unique and historically important venue, which has towers and turrets and evidence of its original drawbridge. The hotel also has The Orangery Restaurant which offers a relaxed addition to the hotel and an award-winning spa with far reaching views over the River Esk.

Part of The Robert Parker Collection of hotels, Dalhousie Castle offers not only a magical Scottish experience, but also a glimpse into the country's fascinating heritage.

Dalhousie Castle, shrouded in history and mystery, its rich atmosphere permeates your being - savour the essence of Scotland's past, present and future and enliven your senses.

PRESSED GUINEA FOWL

SERVES 4

 A light unoaked Chardonnay or Anjou Rosé.

Ingredients

Pressed Guinea Fowl

1 guinea fowl
300g duck fat
1 carrot (washed, roughly chopped)
1 leek (washed, roughly chopped)
2 sticks celery (washed, roughly chopped)
2 sprigs thyme
2 bay leaves
4 sprigs tarragon
2 shallots (finely chopped)
2 leaves gelatine (softened in cold water)

Pickled Girolles

200g girolles
100ml vinegar
100ml water
20g sugar
2 sprigs thyme
2 cloves garlic (chopped)
1 shallot (finely chopped)

Method

For The Pressed Guinea Fowl (Prepare ahead)

Preheat the oven to 150°C (fan).

Remove the legs from the bird and place in a small pan with the duck fat. Cover and transfer to the oven for 2 hours until the meat is almost falling off the bone.

Put the crown in a large pan and cover with water. Add the roughly chopped vegetables to the pan along with the thyme, bay leaves and half the tarragon. Cook on a simmering boil for 1 hour. Remove the meat, pass the stock through a sieve, reduce down to 200ml, then stir in the softened gelatine. Leave to cool.

Chop the remaining tarragon and sweat with the shallots. Pick the meat from the legs and crown. You will need 2 trays of roughly the same size that fit inside one another. Line the larger tray with a double layer of cling film. Mix the picked meat with the softened shallot. Place in the larger tray and cover with the reduced stock. Cover with cling film, chill for 20 minutes, then top with the other tray. Weigh it down with some cans and refrigerate overnight.

For The Pickled Girolles (Prepare ahead)

Clean the girolles thoroughly and drain well. Boil the vinegar and water with the sugar, thyme, garlic and shallot, then pour over the girolles immediately. Leave to cool. Chill overnight.

Chef's Tip

Small girolles work best as they will have little water in them. If you only have large ones, then it would be best to fry them off first adding a little salt to render out the water, then add to the *liquor*.

To Serve

Carefully lift the top tray off the pressed guinea fowl, remove the cling film and flip over onto a board. Remove the bottom tray holding onto the cling film and discard. Slice and serve as pictured with the pickled girolles.

PORK BELLY, LANGOUSTINE, TROMPETTE

SERVES 4

A French Viognier, New Zealand Marlborough or an Italian Primitivo.

Ingredients

Pork Belly

800g pork belly
2 sprigs thyme
2 bay leaves
1 whole star anise
10 coriander seeds
60g Maldon salt flakes
500g duck fat

Potatoes

4 large Rooster potatoes
duck fat (reserved from the pork belly)

Langoustines And Sauce

8 Scottish langoustines
2 shallots (sliced)
2 sprigs thyme
200ml white wine
300ml double cream

Mushrooms

5 ceps
20g black trompette mushrooms
1 shallot (roughly chopped)
dry white wine (splash of)
100ml cream

Method

For The Pork Belly (Prepare ahead)

Trim any top skin off the pork and remove any bones. Blitz the herbs and spices in a blender, then add the salt and give it a quick burst; you don't want the salt to be too fine. Rub the salt mix into the pork and leave for 2 hours or overnight.

Preheat the oven to 160°C (fan).

Rinse the pork, then cook in the duck fat, covered with foil, for 2 hours. Allow to cool for 30 minutes in the fat, then remove and cool on a tray. When cold, cut into dice. Do not discard the fat.

For The Potatoes

Cut the potatoes into 2½cm dice. Cook in the duck fat for 25 minutes until cooked through, then drain.

For The Langoustines And Sauce

Put a large pan of water on to boil. Remove the tails, then stick a toothpick through each tail to help keep them straight.
Pop into the boiling water for 30 seconds, then refresh in ice. Peel the shells.

Put the shallots and langoustine heads in a hot pan and fry, adding the thyme, then the white wine. Reduce by half, then add water so that it just about covers the langoustines. Reduce by half, then add the cream and reduce again by half. Blitz this, then strain. If you don't have a suitable blender, bash the shells with a rolling pin before putting in the pan to extract as much flavour and meat from the claws.

For The Mushrooms

Simply wash the trompettes in water and drain well. The ceps absorb water almost like a sponge so these are best washed with a paint brush and water! Keep 2 nice slices to fry per portion. Sweat off the shallot, then add the ceps and fry. *Deglaze* with a little white wine, then add the cream. Heat through, then blitz.

To Serve

Place the pork, fat-side down, in a dry frying pan and crisp up. Colour the potatoes, then turn the pork over, reduce the heat and add a little duck fat to heat up slowly. Add the cep slices. The langoustines need 30 seconds on each side in foaming butter. Serve as pictured.

Chef's Tip

It's best to prep this the day before so all you have to do is finish it off.

PISTACHIO LINZER TORTE

SERVES 4-6

🍷 *Try a straw wine (Vin Jaune) or an IPA well chilled for something different.*

Ingredients

Sweet Pastry

100g butter
100g icing sugar
250g plain flour
1 tsp pistachio paste
1 egg yolk
1 medium egg

Raspberry Jam

250g raspberries
250g caster sugar
1 lime (zest and lime of)

Pistachio Cream Filling

60g butter
60g caster sugar
45g pistachios (finely chopped)
2 tsp pistachio paste
20g plain flour
1 egg yolk
1 medium egg

Garnish

raspberries

4-6 individual or 1 large tart case (greased)

Method

For The Sweet Pastry

Cream the butter and sugar together, then add the flour and pistachio paste. Mix in the eggs to form a dough and chill for 30 minutes.

Preheat the oven to 165°C (fan).

Roll the pastry out to 2mm thickness and line the tart cases. Bake for 12 minutes, then leave to rest and cool.

For The Raspberry Jam

Put the raspberries and sugar in a pan with the lime zest and juice. Cook until the sugar has dissolved and the raspberries have broken down to a 'jammy' consistency. Set aside to cool.

For The Pistachio Cream Filling

Cream the butter and sugar together, then add the finely chopped pistachios and paste. Stir in the flour, then the eggs. Chill the mix filling for 10 minutes, then transfer to a piping bag to make it easier to fill the tart cases.

Chef's Tip

The greener the pistachios the better the flavour and presentation.

To Finish

Preheat the oven to 170°C (fan).

Spread a little jam over the bases of the cold pastry cases. Pipe the pistachio cream in, leaving a 5mm gap to the top of the tart as the cream will rise slightly. Bake for 12-15 minutes until golden brown. Leave to cool, then carefully spread another thin layer of jam on top. Garnish with fresh raspberries.

EAT ON THE GREEN

Udny Green, Ellon, Aberdeenshire, AB41 7RS

01651 842 337
www.eatonthegreen.co.uk Twitter: eatonthegreen1 Facebook: Eat On The Green

Cooking without the finest ingredients in the world is like trying to prepare a three course meal with one hand tied behind your back. It's probably going to taste ok but could be better.

Thankfully, Eat on the Green 'Kilted Chef' Craig Wilson likes to use both hands when he's in the kitchen and has an uncompromising desire to use only the freshest, finest ingredients. Craig doesn't need to look far from his North East home for inspiration as the Aberdeenshire food larder is packed with quality raw produce and products that have put the region on the international culinary map. From fresh seafood caught in the North Sea, to Scotch Beef PGI and Scotch Lamb PGI, not forgetting the wide range of vegetables and fruit grown in the vast Aberdeenshire countryside.

Foodies from throughout the world are discovering the unique flavours and unmistakable quality of the North East of Scotland through world-renowned food and drink brands like Walkers Shortbread, BrewDog and Mackie's Ice Cream, not to mention the vast selection of whisky distilleries and the growing popularity of gin producers, which are often regarded as some of the best in the world.

Chefs in kitchens located throughout the upper east side of Scotland don't just produce food, they produce immersive experiences that have the ability to translate into a thousand languages and inspire locals and visitors alike. This is food at its very best; this is Aberdeenshire.

The Gin Garden

After 30 years in the industry, 'Kilted Chef' Craig Wilson has received wide recognition from local and national awards and was recently inducted into the Masterchefs of Great Britain.

EAT on the GREEN

AILSA CRAIG GOAT'S CHEESE CHEESECAKE, WALKERS THREE SEED OATCAKE BRITTLE, BEETROOT, HONEY

SERVES 4

 Tanqueray Gin & Basil Tonic.

Ingredients

Goat's Cheese Cheesecake

230g Ailsa Craig goat's cheese
2 tsp Scottish heather honey
120g crème fraîche
sea salt (pinch of)

Pickled Beetroot

60g home grown beetroot
250g sugar
500ml white wine vinegar
1 bay leaf
1 sprig thyme

Walkers Three Seed Oatcake Brittle

150g Walkers three seed oatcakes
300g sugar

Salad Garnish

20g mizuna, wild rocket, home grown salad leaves
rapeseed oil (drizzle of)

4 plain cookie cutters

Method

For The Goat's Cheese Cheesecake

Mix the goat's cheese together with the honey and half the crème fraîche. Add a pinch of sea salt.

For The Pickled Beetroot

Place all the ingredients into a medium-sized saucepan, bring to the boil and simmer for 1½ hours. Remove from the pan, dice the beetroot and return it to the pickling *liquor.*

For The Walkers Three Seed Oatcake Brittle

Place the oatcakes in a food processor and blitz until it resembles a coarse crumb. Add the crumb and sugar to a heavy-based pan and stir for 7-8 minutes until the sugar is warmed through and combined well with the oatcake crumb. Transfer to a baking tray lined with parchment, place another sheet of paper on top and press down. Once set, break it by hand to create the brittle.

Chef's Tip

Lightly bake the oatcakes for a toasted flavour.

To Assemble

Lay a cookie cutter onto each plate and place the oat brittle into the bottom of the cutter. Fill this with the goat's cheese and honey mixture. Top with the remaining crème fraîche, followed by the diced beetroot. Remove the cutter, arrange the summer salad leaves on top and add the diced beetroot around the base of the cheesecake. Drizzle a small amount of rapeseed oil on the leaves.

UDNY GARDEN HERB CRUSTED SCOTCH LAMB, GARLIC NEW TATTIES

SERVES 4

🍷 *BrewDog Vagabond*
This local gluten-free pale ale partners well with this dish.

Ingredients

Garden Herb Breadcrumbs

2-3 slices bread
sea salt (large pinch of)
25g fresh garden herbs

Garden Herb Crusted Scotch Lamb

1 Scotch lamb loin eye
4 free-range egg whites (beaten)
100g fresh garden herb breadcrumbs
rapeseed oil (drizzle of)

Garlic Herb Butter

1 clove garlic
4 stalks parsley (picked)
1 sprig thyme (picked)
1 sprig rosemary (picked)
50g Scottish salted butter
sea salt (pinch of)

Garlic New Tatties

500g Jazzy Aberdeenshire new season tatties
sea salt

Crispy Kale

black kale
oil (to fry)
salt (pinch of)

To Serve

4 large fresh chard leaves (washed)
4 fresh spinach leaves (washed)

Method

For The Garden Herb Breadcrumbs

Blitz the bread on its own in a food processor to make the breadcrumbs. Add the fresh garden herbs and salt and blitz until it resembles a fine crumb.

For The Garden Herb Crusted Scotch Lamb

Trim the lamb loin eye, dip into the beaten egg white, then into the garden herb crumb and place on kitchen paper. Preheat a non-stick frying pan with a generous splash of rapeseed oil, then gently place the crusted lamb into the hot oil, turning after 2 minutes until both sides are golden. Remove from the pan and leave to rest on a cooling rack before carving.

For The Garlic Herb Butter

Roughly chop the garlic, parsley, thyme and rosemary. Add the butter and sea salt and gently melt on a low heat to infuse the flavours. Correct the seasoning if necessary.

For The Garlic New Tatties

Gently wash the new tatties, place in a saucepan with a sprinkle of sea salt and any remaining herbs and simmer for approximately 10 minutes until tender. Drain from the water and lightly toss in the garlic herb butter.

For The Crispy Kale

Wash and dry the kale. Shallow or deep fry (185ºC) for a couple of minutes until crispy. Place on kitchen paper and sprinkle with a pinch of salt.

To Assemble

Place the spinach and chard on a rustic sharing platter and place the garlic new tatties on the leaves. Lay the carved, crusted lamb on the tatties and dress all with the remaining garlic butter.

> **Chef's Tip**
> Use a food processor to make breadcrumbs, then leave on a tray to dry out for a few hours before coating the lamb.

GLENGARIOCH WASHED CHOCOLATE, ABERDEENSHIRE BARRA RASPBERRIES, MACKIE'S TRADITIONAL DAIRY ICE CREAM

SERVES 4

 Old Fashioned Aberdeenshire raspberry lemonade, adding a dram of whisky if the mood takes you.

Ingredients

Brownie Base

5 eggs
400g caster sugar
200g flour
220g Valrhona dark chocolate (70%)
220g Scottish butter
sea salt (pinch of)

Chocolate Ganache

700g Valrhona dark chocolate (70%)
350g Scottish butter (small dice)
sea salt (pinch of)
90g heather honey
800ml Scottish double cream

Raspberry Purée

100g Aberdeenshire Barra raspberries
50g sugar
½ lemon (juice of)

Whisky Wash

100ml Glengarioch whisky
70g caster sugar

To Serve

Mackie's Traditional dairy ice cream
Aberdeenshire raspberries
edible flowers

1cm deep baking tray (lined with parchment)

Chef's Tip

Ensure each ingredient purchased is of the finest quality as the flavours will be equally complementary when served.

Method

For The Brownie Base

Preheat the oven to 180°C.

Whisk the eggs and sugar until light and fluffy. Sift the flour and add to the egg mixture. Melt the chocolate and butter in a pan, add the sea salt and mix well into the egg mixture. Pour into the prepared tin. Bake for 20 minutes. When cooling, place parchment with another tray on top and a weight to condense the brownie.

For The Chocolate Ganache

Put the chocolate in a bowl with the butter, salt and honey. Bring the cream to the boil, pour over the chocolate and mix until all lumps are gone. Pour over the cooled brownie and leave.

For The Raspberry Purée

Gently simmer the fresh raspberries and sugar with the juice of half a lemon. Pour through a fine sieve and chill.

For The Whisky Wash

Simmer the whisky and sugar together for a few minutes. Leave to cool.

To Assemble

Neatly cut strips of the ganache covered brownie and place in the centre of the plates garnishing with the raspberries, purée and edible flowers.

Add a generous scoop of Mackie's Traditional dairy ice cream. Pour the whisky wash into a small atomiser and lightly spray over the chocolate ganache and raspberries.

106
FHIOR RESTAURANT

36 Broughton Street, Edinburgh, EH1 3SB

0131 477 5000
www.fhior.com Facebook: @FhiorRestaurant

Created by chef Scott Smith and his wife Laura, Fhior's approach is ultra-seasonal and naturally innovative; combining contrasting flavours, textures and temperatures with a focus that's firmly on the produce.

Fhior takes you on a journey through the flavours of Scotland's seasonal larder with exquisite ingredient-led dishes presented in enticing set menus, designed to provoke the palate and create an unforgettable dining experience.

The frequently changing seasonal menu will let you discover ancient grains, heritage varieties and foraged ingredients alongside the freshest of produce presented in creative and inspiring dishes that regularly include traditional techniques such as fermentation, infusion, cultures and pickling.

The wine selection sits snugly alongside this ethos, showcasing a selection from around the world that focuses on the craft and expertise of the winemaker. All wines show skill, minimal intervention and interest.

The restaurant itself is simple and modern with neutral hues, a relaxed atmosphere and artwork with a sense of humour. This is all paired with upbeat music and informal but informative service to make you feel like all the details are covered without it being too serious.

Located in the heart of Edinburgh on Broughton Street, Fhior is a dining experience that combines the essence of Scotland and the flair of one of the UK's most exciting young chefs.

Fhior, meaning 'true' in Gaelic, pays tribute to Scotland's rich food landscape and heritage by showcasing its outstanding natural produce, both wild and cultivated, driving a truly creative dining experience.

LOBSTER, RHUBARB, SEA SANDWORT

SERVES 4

 Tierra del Itata Muscat 2016 Christelle Guibert, Itata Valley (Chile)

Ingredients

Lobster Sauce

700g lobster (live)
iced water (enough to cover the whole lobster)
150g butter

Cucumber And Rhubarb

1 small cucumber
1 stalk rhubarb
salt

To Serve

20g sea sandwort

Method

For The Lobster Sauce

Bring a pan of salted water to a rapid boil (large enough to fit the lobster in and cover fully). Put the lobster in and cook for 6 minutes. Drop into iced water to halt the cooking. Remove the meat from the claws and tail and refrigerate.

Put the lobster shells and trimmings in a saucepan and cover with water. Bring to the boil and simmer for 3 hours skimming off any impurities as they float to the surface.

Strain the shells and discard, then return the cooking juices to the heat to reduce by three-quarters.

Add the butter gradually and whisk to *emulsify*. Keep warm.

For The Cucumber And Rhubarb

Place the whole cucumber on a barbecue to char the outside. Cut into quarters lengthways and remove the seeds. Slice and season.

Slice the rhubarb very thinly and lightly salt for 1 hour.

To Plate

Gently warm the lobster in the butter sauce. Divide the lobster into 4 portions and place in the centre of the plates. Top with the rhubarb, cucumber and sea sandwort, dress with the butter sauce.

Chef's Tip

Borage can be a replacement for sea sandwort.

CHICKEN, LOVAGE, CHICKEN OF THE WOODS

SERVES 4

*Saint-Aubin 1er Cru Sous Roche Dumay 2012
Bernard Moreau Burgundy (France)*

Ingredients

Lovage Mayonnaise
250ml vegetable oil
100g lovage
2 egg yolks
40ml cider vinegar

Barley
200g pearl barley
800ml seasoned water
butter (small knob of)
20g lovage (chopped)

Chicken
4 chicken breasts (skin on)
1 litre dark chicken stock
oil (drizzle of)
salt (to season)
butter (knob of)

Mushrooms
100g chicken of the woods mushrooms
(roughly chopped)
butter (knob of)
salt and pepper

Method

For The Lovage Mayonnaise
Warm the oil to 70°C and blend with the lovage. Strain in muslin and collect the green oil. Whisk the egg yolks and cider vinegar. Slowly add the lovage oil to make a mayonnaise.

For The Barley
Cook the barley in the seasoned water until tender and cooked. Strain and set aside.

For The Chicken
Trim the chicken breasts. Cook the trimmings in a pan until browned, then add the chicken stock. Reduce by half or until thickened.

Preheat the oven to 210°C.

Cook the chicken in a hot pan with a little oil, skin-side down, until the skin is crisp and golden. Season with salt. Add the butter to the pan, turn the chicken over and place in the oven for 6-8 minutes until just cooked. Allow to rest for 5 minutes.

To Serve
Reheat the barley with a small amount of butter and add the chopped lovage. Place the barley on the plate.

Sauté the roughly chopped chicken of the woods mushrooms with a little butter and season. Place on top of the barley. Add the lovage mayonnaise to the plate, sit the chicken next to the barley and mushrooms and sauce with the reduced stock.

Chef's Tip
Finish the dish with crispy chicken skin to enhance the roasted chicken flavour.

STRAWBERRY, WOODRUFF, RAPESEED

SERVES 4

 Cuvée Spätlese 2013 Kracher Burgenland (Austria)

Ingredients

Woodruff Ice Cream

375ml whole milk
250ml double cream
50g woodruff
iced water
50g caster sugar
3 egg yolks (75g)

Strawberries

500g fresh strawberries
20g caster sugar
10ml white wine vinegar
1½g agar agar

To Serve

15g dried rapeseeds
50ml rapeseed oil (cold pressed)
woodruff flowers

Method

For The Woodruff Ice Cream

Bring the milk and cream to the boil, then remove from the heat. Blend in the woodruff and set aside to infuse for 2 minutes. Strain it into a bowl set over iced water to halt the cooking and preserve the colour.

Whisk the sugar and egg yolks until creamy, then slowly pour in the woodruff cream. Heat to 75°C, then leave to cool. Churn in an ice cream machine.

Chef's Tip

Use gorse if you are unable to get woodruff flowers. Gorse flowers, available all year, can have similar grassy notes.

For The Strawberries

Slice 100g of the strawberries. Chop the remaining 400g and mix with the sugar. Tie in a muslin cloth and allow the juice to drip out. Measure out 100ml of strawberry juice and add the vinegar. Add the agar agar and bring to the boil whilst whisking. Boil gently for 3 minutes and allow to set. Once cold, use a hand blender to blend into a gel.

To Plate

Scoop the woodruff ice cream into an open bowl and carefully place the sliced strawberries on top. Add dots of the strawberry gel and drizzle with the rapeseed oil, adding a pinch of rapeseeds. Finish with woodruff flowers if available.

116
KATE'S OF INVERURIE

Inverurie, Aberdeenshire

07873 633 360
www.katesinverurie.com Twitter: @kates_inverurie

Kate's is a family business run by chef Liam McKenna and his wife Kate. It was started in response to what they saw as the changing restaurant scene in the area and the demand for personal dining experiences in unique locations. The core of their business is exceptional food and the approach is simple, use the best produce Scotland's larder has to offer and showcase it in their menus.

Being an outside caterer allows people to enjoy restaurant quality food in a surrounding of their choosing. From stately homes and castles to tipis and dining al fresco in secluded locations, the possibilities for customising dining experiences are endless. The flexibility of both the location and menu lead to the creation of truly unique events.

Kate's

PEA MOUSSE
Parmesan crisp, pickled mushrooms

LOBSTER RAVIOLI
Buttered spinach, lobster bisque

PAN ROAST GRESSINGHAM DUCK BREAST
Braised leg & foie gras bon bon, pickled cherries,
celeriac

RASPBERRY SOUFFLE
Barra Berry raspberry souffle, raspberry sorbet

Making use of the amazing produce and suppliers that Aberdeenshire has to offer, Kate's creates personalised menus tailored to individual events. Delivering a fine dining experience in unique locations across Scotland.

THE TEASMITH GIN & TONIC TAY SALMON

SERVES 4

*The Teasmith Gin, served with premium tonic
water and garnished with a spring of mint and
plenty of ice.*

Ingredients

Salmon

300g Scottish salmon (skinned, pin boned)
100ml Teasmith gin
50g sea salt
20g sugar

Avocado Purée

3 avocados
1 lemon (juice of)

Compressed Tonic Cucumber

1 cucumber
½ bottle Fever Tree tonic

Garnish

1 apple (cut into strips)
caviar
micro parsley
salt (to season)

Method

For The Salmon

Prepare the salmon by cutting it in half lengthways. Mix the gin, salt and sugar well in a non-reactive container. Add the salmon pieces and cover in the gin mix. Cover and place in the refrigerator for 30-40 minutes, turning halfway through.

Remove the salmon from the gin mix and rinse under cold water. Pat dry between paper towels. Cut into 4 strips roughly 2½cm wide.

For The Avocado Purée

Peel the avocados and blend with the lemon juice until smooth.

For The Compressed Tonic Cucumber

Cut the cucumber into rectangles roughly 6cm x 2cm in size. Place into a food saver tub with the tonic. Remove the air using a food saver machine which compresses the tonic into the cucumber. Leave to marinate for 2 hours, then remove from the bag and blow torch the surface until blackened.

Chef's Tip

If you do not have a blow torch to hand, you can place the top of the cucumber in a hot dry pan until coloured.

To Assemble

Place the salmon to the side of the plate. Spoon the avocado onto the salmon and arrange the apple, caviar and parsley on top. Finish by adding the cucumber to the plate beside the salmon.

CHICKEN, WILD MUSHROOMS, CAVOLO NERO

SERVES 4

 Chivite Finca Villatuerta Chardonnay, Navarra (Spain)

Ingredients

Chicken Breasts

5 Gartmorn Farm free-range chicken breasts (skin on)
1 egg yolk
200ml double cream
150g wild mushrooms (washed, chopped)

Carrot Purée

200g carrots
10g butter
100ml double cream

Chicken Wings

4 Gartmorn Farm free-range chicken wings
20g plain flour
20g eggs (beaten)
20g breadcrumbs
300ml vegetable oil

Wild Mushrooms

16 Chanterelle mushrooms
20g butter

Cavolo Nero

4 stems cavolo nero (ripped into 12 pieces)
300ml vegetable oil
salt (to season)

Chef's Tip

When frying cavolo nero, cover the pan loosely with a lid as the moisture from the leaves can cause the oil to splash.

Method

For The Chicken Breasts

Preheat the oven to 180°C (fan).

Remove the skin from the breasts and place on a tray between 2 sheets of non-stick paper. Cover the surface with a heatproof weight and bake for 10-15 minutes. Cool, then break up into pieces.

Chop one of the breasts into 2cm cubes and blend in a food processor with the egg and cream until smooth. Stir in the mushrooms and season.

Bring a large pot of water to the boil. Butterfly open the 4 remaining breasts and fill with the chicken mix. Roll into cylinders using cling film and seal with a knot at each end. Place into the pan of boiling water, then remove from the heat and cover with a lid. Leave to cook slowly for around 45 minutes.

For The Carrot Purée

Peel and thinly chop the carrots. Warm the butter in a pan, add the carrots and cook over a low heat until beginning to soften, then add the cream and cook until soft. Blend in a food processor to a smooth purée, season and set aside.

For The Chicken Wings

Bone out the chicken wings, removing the second small bone. Clean the bone removing all the sinew. Roll the meat into a ball using cling film and tie securely. Poach in simmering water for 10-15 minutes. Once cool, remove the wings from the cling film and crumb by first rolling in flour, followed by the beaten egg mix and finally the breadcrumbs. Insert a cleaned bone into each ball and shallow fry in the oil until golden brown.

For The Wild Mushrooms

Lightly fry the mushrooms in butter, season.

For The Cavolo Nero

Heat the oil to 170°C. Add the cavolo nero and fry until crispy. Set aside on absorbent paper towel.

To Assemble

Remove the breasts from the cling film, cut into 3 pieces and position on the plate. Add a chicken wing and 2 generous spoonfuls of carrot purée. Finish with the broken up crispy chicken skin and crispy cavolo nero.

ETON MESS PANNA COTTA

SERVES 4

 Classic French Martini

Ingredients

Raspberry Purée

1kg raspberries
300g caster sugar
lemon juice (squeeze of)

Meringue

80g caster sugar
80g egg whites
50g raspberry purée

Panna Cotta

500ml double cream
275ml whole milk
30g caster sugar
1 vanilla pod (seeds of)
4 leaves gelatine (soaked in cold water)

Raspberry Jelly

500g raspberry purée
25ml Chambord
40g caster sugar
4 leaves gelatine (soaked in cold water)

Raspberry Sorbet

450g raspberry purée
80g caster sugar
30ml water

Chantilly Cream

150ml double cream
50g caster sugar
1 vanilla pod (seeds of)

Garnish

12 fresh raspberries

20cm x 10cm container (lined with cling film)
3 baking trays (lined with greaseproof paper)

Method

For The Raspberry Purée

Place the ingredients in a pan and gently heat to a low simmer.
Blend and pass through a fine sieve, reserving the smooth purée.

For The Meringue (Prepare ahead)

Preheat the oven to 50°C (fan).

Whisk the sugar and eggs together until thick and smooth.
The meringue should be glossy and hold its shape. Divide evenly
into 3 separate bowls. Leaving one bowl plain, add the raspberry
purée to the other 2 bowls in varying amounts so that one is a
darker shade of pink than the other. Smooth each mix onto a
separate baking tray in a thin layer and place in the oven for
6 hours or until completely dry. Break into shards.

For The Panna Cotta

Combine the cream, milk, sugar and vanilla in a pan and gently
heat until the sugar is dissolved. Squeeze any excess water
from the gelatine leaves and add to the cream mix, stirring until
dissolved. Pass through a fine sieve and set aside.

For The Raspberry Jelly

Warm the raspberry purée in a pan with the Chambord and
sugar until the sugar has dissolved. Add the drained gelatine
leaves and stir until dissolved. Pass through a fine sieve.

To Create The Layered Panna Cotta

Pour a 2mm layer of the raspberry jelly into the lined container
and leave to set in the refrigerator. Once set, layer with 2mm of
panna cotta mix and leave to set. Repeat the process,
alternating between the raspberry jelly and the panna cotta
until you have 7 layers.

For The Raspberry Sorbet

Warm all the ingredients together over a low heat until the sugar
has dissolved, then pass through a fine sieve. Once cool, churn in
an ice-cream machine and place in the freezer until required.

For The Chantilly Cream

Whisk the cream, sugar and vanilla until soft peaks form.

To Serve

Cut the set panna cotta into 4 rectangles, 6cm x 2cm, and
arrange on separate plates. On top of each slice, place 1 spoon
of sorbet and 2 spoons of Chantilly cream. Garnish with fresh
raspberries and the meringue shards. Serve immediately.

Chef's Tip

Heat up the knife in boiling water before cutting the panna
cotta to achieve a smooth finish.

126
LA POTINIERE

Main Street, Gullane, EH31 2AA

01620 843 214
www.lapotiniere.co.uk Twitter: @LaPotGullane

La Potinière, situated in Gullane's Main Street only 30 minutes from Edinburgh has, over the years, become known for offering a warm and friendly welcome to those wishing to dine exceptionally well within a relaxed atmosphere. Since July 2002, La Potinière has been run by Mary Runciman and Keith Marley, both individually award-winning chefs.

Their hard work and consistency has not gone unnoticed, being awarded Newcomer of the Year for Scotland in the Good Food Guide in 2004. La Potinière has been awarded Best Fine Dining in East Lothian along with Best Front of House twice. In 2008 they saw their first entry into the Michelin Guide and have remained in each edition since. In 2015 Keith was awarded Pastry Chef of the Year for Scotland.

The menu changes regularly according to availability of the best produce throughout the seasons, some of which comes from its very own restaurant garden. Along with a small but comprehensive wine list, La Potinière ensures a memorable culinary experience.

La Potinière is surrounded by some of Scotland's finest golf courses including Gullane's renowned Links and the world famous Muirfield, home to 'The Open' and, since their time in Gullane, Mary and Keith have built up a regular, local, golfing clientele and have many loyal customers from further afield.

They feel so lucky to be in such a beautiful location with fabulous scenery, beaches and of course a rich supply of the finest ingredients Scotland has to offer, right on their doorstep.

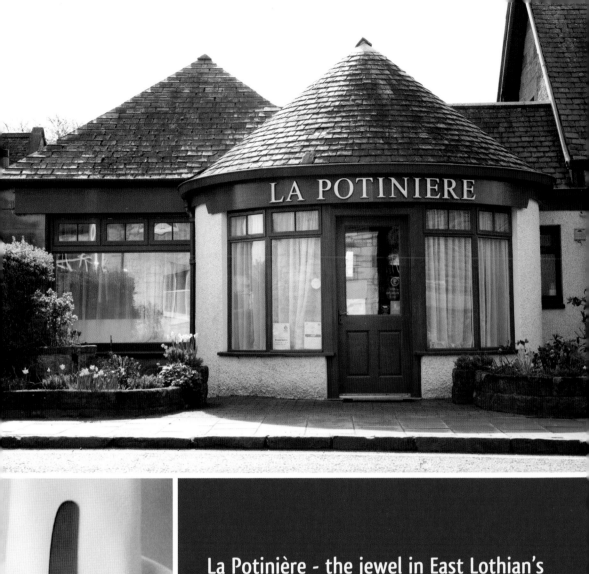

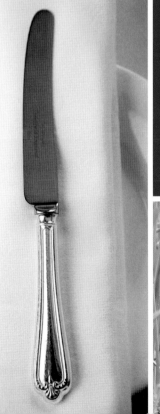

La Potinière - the jewel in East Lothian's culinary crown.

SCALLOP & LANGOUSTINE CEVICHE, AVOCADO MOUSSE, SUMMER SALAD, LEMON DRESSING

SERVES 4

 Ca Di Alte Prosecco Spumante Extra Dry (Italy) or Christophe Denizot, Le Vieux Château, Premier Cru, Montagny Blanc 2015 (France)

Ingredients

Avocado Mousse

1 large avocado
15ml lemon juice
30g natural Greek yoghurt
salt and pepper

Scallop And Langoustine Ceviche

4 fresh large scallops (shelled, cleaned)
4 fresh langoustines (shelled, cleaned)
10ml lime juice

Lemon Dressing

1 lemon (zest and juice of)
1-2 tbsp rapeseed oil

To Serve

5g chives (chopped)
5g chervil (chopped)
salt and pepper
12 melon balls
12 x ½cm watermelon dice
6 asparagus tips (*blanched*)
30g peas (*blanched,* seasoned)
crispy pea shoots
dried scallop roe powder

Method

For The Avocado Mousse

Blend the avocado with the lemon juice until smooth. Stir in the Greek yoghurt and season, chill.

For The Scallop And Langoustine Ceviche

Dice the scallops and langoustines. Carefully mix with the lime juice, then chill for 20-30 minutes.

For The Lemon Dressing

Whisk the lemon zest and juice with the rapeseed oil to a viscous consistency. Check the acidity and adjust the seasoning.

To Finish And Serve

Mix the herbs with the scallops and langoustines and season.

Pipe the avocado mousse onto the plates and arrange the melon, peas, asparagus and pea shoots. Plate the scallop mix, add the lemon dressing and dust with scallop powder. Serve immediately.

Chef's Tip

Keep the mousse well chilled and tightly covered to prevent oxidisation. The langoustines and scallops can be seared or grilled instead to add a warm element to the plate.

POACHED & SEARED LOIN OF SMOKED PORK, SLOW COOKED SHOULDER BON BON, PICKLED CABBAGE & CARROT, PORK & GINGER JUS

SERVES 4

🍷 *Willy Gisselbrecht, Gewurztraminer 2015 (France)*

Ingredients

Pickled Cabbage And Carrot

10g caster sugar
5g salt
100ml rice vinegar
5g caraway seeds (ground in a pestle and mortar)
200g white cabbage (finely shredded/*julienne*)
75g carrot (*julienne*)

Pork Bon Bon

170g slow cooked pork shoulder (reserve cooking juices for sauce)
75g Granny Smith apple (peeled, diced, *blanched*)
20g stem ginger in syrup (puréed)
seasoned flour, egg, panko breadcrumbs (to *pane*)

Potatoes

500g new potatoes
50g butter (melted)
salt and pepper

Pork Loins And Ginger Jus

2 small pork loins, trimmed, smoked (reserve trimmings for sauce)
100ml white wine
15ml balsamic vinegar
1 small onion (sliced)
1 small carrot (chopped)
1 stick celery (chopped)
2 cloves garlic (chopped)
reserved slow cooked pork juices
10g fresh ginger (grated)
salt

To Serve

seasonal vegetables

Method

For The Pickled Cabbage And Carrot (Prepare the day before)

Dissolve the sugar and salt in the vinegar, add the ground caraway. Pour onto the cabbage and carrot, then toss together. Chill for 24 hours.

> **Chef's Tip**
>
> Do not overheat the cabbage so as to keep it crisp and retain the freshness of the dish.

For The Pork Bon Bon

Chop or shred the meat and mix with the apple and ginger. Check the seasoning and consistency. Form balls and chill.

When chilled, *pane* with flour, egg and breadcrumbs. Refrigerate.

For The Potatoes

Cook the potatoes, then skin and slice 2-3mm thick. Fan into a 7-8cm ring forming a disc, brush with the butter, season and reserve in the fridge.

For The Pork Loins And Ginger Jus

Vacuum the pork loins and poach for 2 hours at 55ºC. Alternatively, pan fry the loins in a little oil and butter.

Brown the reserved trimmings until golden, then add the wine and vinegar. Reduce, then add the chopped onion, carrot, celery and garlic. Sweat until softened, then pour in the pork juices and reduce to a sauce consistency. Pass through a sieve, then season to taste with ginger and salt.

To Assemble

Preheat the oven to 180ºC (fan).

Warm the potato discs in the oven for 20 minutes. Deep fry the bon bon (170ºC) for 6-8 minutes. Gently warm the pickled vegetables. Remove the loins from the bags and pat dry. Season, then sear in a hot pan. Plate the potato with the cabbage on top, then set a bon bon on top. Slice the loin and arrange as pictured. Serve with the vegetables and jus.

COCONUT MACARON WITH CHOCOLATE & ORANGE CREME PATISSIERE, FRUITS, ORANGE SORBET

SERVES 8

Coteaux Du Layon 1er Cru, 2014, Domaine Des Forges (France)

Ingredients

Coconut Macaron

100g dessicated coconut
100g icing sugar
92g egg whites
100g caster sugar, 25ml water
toasted dessicated coconut (for sprinkling)

Orange Sorbet

250ml fresh orange juice
1 orange (finely grated zest of)
½ lemon (juice of)
85g icing sugar

Chocolate And Orange Crème Patissiere

125ml whole milk
½ vanilla pod
25g caster sugar
30g egg yolk (about 1 large egg yolk)
27g flour
15g cocoa powder
1 large orange (grated zest of)
80ml whipping cream (lightly whipped)

Passion Fruit Gel

120ml 1:1 stock syrup
3g agar agar
120ml passion fruit juice

Fresh Fruit And Fruit Coulis

½ ripe pineapple (peeled, trimmed, sliced)
1 mango (peeled, trimmed, diced)
1:1 stock syrup (as required)
1-2 tbsp fresh orange juice (if required)
1 kiwi fruit (peeled, trimmed, sliced)
12 raspberries (halved)

Garnish

micro mint, chocolate shards and curls

Method

For The Coconut Macaron

Blend the coconut and icing sugar to a fine powder, then add 55g of the egg whites to the powder.

Boil the caster sugar and water to 118°C.

Whip the remaining egg whites in a mixer. Slowly add the hot sugar mix and continue to whip until it cools to 50°C. Fold the meringue into the coconut mixture until you have a dropping consistency. Pipe onto silicone mats, sprinkle with coconut and leave for 30 minutes to form a skin.

Preheat the oven to 140°C (fan). Bake for 12 minutes, then leave to cool. Store in an airtight container in the freezer.

> **Chef's Tip**
> Make sure the coconut and icing sugar are well blended. Use 3 to 4 day old egg whites at room temperature. Ensure the bases are well formed for releasing from the mats.

For The Sorbet

Combine all the ingredients and stir well. Churn in an ice cream machine and reserve in the freezer.

For The Chocolate And Orange Crème Patissiere

Boil the milk and vanilla. Cream the egg yolks and caster sugar together. Sieve the flour and cocoa powder together, then stir into the egg yolks. Pour the boiling milk onto the yolk mixture, combine well and bring back to the boil. Simmer for 2 minutes, then add the orange zest. Cool, then fold in the whipped cream. Refrigerate.

For The Passion Fruit Gel

Add the syrup to the agar agar and gently simmer, stirring, for 5 minutes. Warm the passion fruit juice but do not boil. Stir the warm juice into the syrup, then pour into a tray and set in the fridge. When set, blend until smooth. Pass through a sieve. Store in a piping bag or sauce bottle in the fridge.

For The Fresh Fruit And Fruit Coulis

Purée the pineapple and mango trimmings together. Add the stock syrup, then pass through a sieve. Add a little stock syrup as needed being careful not to over sweeten. Use orange juice if needed to gain the right consistency.

To Assemble

Pipe the chocolate crème onto the macarons. Arrange the fruit on top and decorate with the passion fruit gel and fruit coulis. *Rocher* the sorbet and garnish with chocolate shards, curls and micro mint. Serve immediately.

136
LE ROI FOU

1 Forth Street, Edinburgh, EH1 3JX

0131 557 9346
www.leroifou.com Twitter: LeRoiFouEdin Facebook: Le Roi Fou Instagram: leroifou_edinburgh

Le Roi Fou in Edinburgh is a relaxed, fine dining restaurant in the vibrant New Town. It is a collaboration between Jérôme Henry and creative director Isolde Nash. Both were drawn to open their first restaurant in Edinburgh due to its outstanding appreciation of food and culture, two of their personal passions.

Over the last 20 years Swiss-French Jérôme has cooked in some of the best kitchens, including seven years as head chef at Anton Mosimann's Private Dining Club in London.

This welcoming restaurant serves modern European dishes influenced by Jérôme's French roots across a variety of dining options, including daily prix fixe, à la carte, tasting and vegetarian. At the centre of most dishes will be the best fresh Scottish produce prepared simply and elegantly, always ensuring that natural flavours are the star of the show.

Consistency of quality is vital, and while they serve some of the great classics and wonderful fresh fish dishes, Jérôme also loves to explore his memories of cooking and eating abroad. Classic dishes such as calves liver are paired with a chimichurri sauce, game such as grouse is served in season, and the best of the sea food is brought to the kitchen daily, with hand-dived scallops being a must.

Le Roi Fou is a neighbourhood restaurant which has a sense of 'home' for people living and working nearby. This award-winning restaurant demonstrates the very best of the European tradition of bars and restaurants where locals dine.

Simplicity, sourcing the best ingredients and consistency are the keys to cooking a good dish.

HERB CRUSTED GLOBE ARTICHOKE, CARROT PUREE BARIGOULE, SUMMER VEGETABLES

SERVES 4

 Loureiro, Dócil, Projecto Dirk Niepoort, Lima Valley, Vinhos Verde, 2017 (Portugal)

Ingredients

Artichokes

100ml olive oil
3 large carrots (peeled, roughly sliced)
2 large red onions (peeled, roughly sliced)
2 stalks celery (washed, sliced)
1 small leek (halved, washed, sliced)
4 large cloves garlic (peeled, sliced)
2 large red chillies (sliced)
10g salt
4 sprigs rosemary, 4 sprigs thyme
1 bunch coriander (stalks only, set tops aside)
2 tsp coriander seeds
1 tsp fennel seeds
1 tsp black peppercorns
100ml white wine, 1½ litres water
4 large globe artichokes

Carrot Purée Barigoule

50ml olive oil
50g butter
500g large good quality carrots (peeled, finely sliced)
2 banana shallots (peeled, sliced)
2 cloves garlic (peeled, sliced)
1 red chilli (halved, deseeded, sliced)
cooking *liquor* from the artichokes
saffron (pinch of)
1 bunch coriander tops, seasoning

Herb Crust

200g parsley (removed from the stalks)
100g watercress, 100g spinach
100g butter (melted)
100g dry breadcrumbs

Summer Vegetable Garnish

12 cherry tomatoes
200g fresh peas, 50g broad beans
8 spears asparagus, 4 radishes (sliced thinly)
olive oil, salt and pepper
12 small basil leaves
fennel fronds (handful of)

Method

For The Artichokes

Place a large pan on a medium heat. Once hot, add the oil, vegetables and salt. Cook until soft then add the herbs and spices. Add the white wine and reduce by half. Pour in the water, bring to the boil, then place the globe artichokes face up in the *liquor*. Cover with a disc of parchment paper and simmer gently for about 30 minutes or until you can pierce the artichokes easily with a knife. Remove the pot from the heat and allow the artichokes to cool in the *liquor*. Using a spoon, scoop out the spines from the artichokes and place into a container. Strain the *liquor*. Cover the artichokes with some *liquor*, reserving the rest for the purée.

For The Carrot Purée Barigoule

Place a medium-sized pan on a medium heat. When warm, add the oil and butter and melt. Add the prepared vegetables to the pan along with a good pinch of salt and pepper. Stir well with a wooden spoon, then allow the vegetables to cook down gently, trying not to colour. Once they've started to soften, add the artichoke *liquor* and saffron, then turn the heat up and simmer until the carrots are very soft and the *liquor* has reduced by half. Transfer to a blender, add the fresh coriander tops and blend on full power until very smooth. Taste for seasoning, then pour into a container and set aside to cool.

For The Herb Crust

Blanch the greens in boiling, salted water for 2 minutes. Strain, then refresh under cold running water. Place the greens into a blender and blitz on full power until smooth. Add the melted butter and blitz again to *emulsify*. Pour the breadcrumbs into a large bowl, then thoroughly fold in the blitzed greens. Spread onto a tray lined with parchment paper and refrigerate. Cut into discs.

To Serve

Preheat the oven to 180ºC.

Cover each artichoke with a disc of the green crust and place on an oven tray. Toss the cherry tomatoes with some olive oil, salt and pepper, then pour them onto the tray alongside the artichokes.

Bake for 10 minutes or until the crust is golden.

Warm the purée in a small saucepan. *Blanch* the summer vegetables in boiling, salted water for 2 minutes. Drain the vegetables, toss in a bowl with olive oil and seasoning.

Dress the plate with a generous spoon of the purée in the centre, place the artichoke on top, then arrange the summer vegetables and *confit* tomatoes around. Sprinkle with the fresh herbs.

GRILLED CALVES LIVER, SMOKED BACON, CHIMICHURRI, RAINBOW CHARD

SERVES 4

🍷 *Syrah Du Maroc, Alain Graillot & Ouled Thaleb, Tandem, 2015 (Morrocco)*

Ingredients

Chimichurri

200g parsley (picked)
100g spinach (picked)
50g oregano (picked)
250ml good olive oil
1 lemon (juice of)
1 tbsp sherry vinegar
chilli powder (pinch of)
seasoning

Rainbow Chard

500g rainbow chard
salt and pepper
olive oil (drizzle of)

Liver And Bacon

4 x180g slices fresh calves liver
12 rashers smoked streaky bacon
salt and pepper
sunflower oil (drizzle of)

Method

For The Chimichurri

Blanch the greens in a pot of salted, boiling water for 2 minutes. Strain, then refresh under cold running water. Transfer to a blender and blitz on full power until smooth. Add a touch of water and olive oil to help *emulsify* the greens. Transfer to a bowl and place in the fridge until needed. The lemon juice, chilli, vinegar and seasoning will be added last minute before serving to ensure the sauce stays vibrant green.

For The Rainbow Chard

Cut the stalks from the rainbow chard leaves and give both a thorough wash. Cut the stalks into finger length batons. Break the leaves apart by hand so they are not too big.

For The Liver And Bacon

Place a griddle pan on a high heat.

Dab the liver dry with some kitchen roll, season with salt and pepper, then rub a little sunflower oil over the surface. Carefully place the liver into the griddle pan and sear until dark. Flip the liver over for just 20 seconds, then remove from the pan and set aside on a tray in a warm place to rest for 5 minutes. Cook the bacon in the liver pan, then add it to the tray with the liver.

To Finish And Serve

While the liver is resting, put the chard stalks in salted boiling water for 1 minute, then add the leaves and cook for a further 1 minute. Drain the chard, place into a bowl and toss with a little olive oil and seasoning. Finish the chimichurri by adding the lemon juice, chilli powder, vinegar and seasoning.

Spoon the chimichurri generously onto the plate, arrange the chard neatly, followed by the bacon and liver. Finish the plate with a drizzle of olive oil and a twist of pepper.

STRAWBERRY, RASPBERRY, SALTED PEANUT CRUMBLE, FRESH GOAT'S CURD

SERVES 4

🍷 *Cerdon, Demi-Sec, Rosé, Bugey, Renardat Fache, Méthode Ancestrale, 2016 (France)*

Ingredients

Salted Peanut Crumble

70g Demerara sugar
50g porridge oats
¼ tsp bicarbonate of soda
50g salted peanuts (chopped)
80g unsalted butter (melted)

Goat's Curd

1 lemon (zest and juice of)
50g icing sugar
250g fresh goat's curd

Berries

800g fresh strawberries
200g fresh raspberries
50g icing sugar
2 tsp good quality balsamic vinegar
1 lemon (juice of)

Method

For The For The Salted Peanut Crumble

Preheat the oven to 170°C.

Weigh all the dry ingredients into a large bowl and rub together with your fingers to ensure everything is well mixed. Add the melted butter and stir thoroughly with a wooden spoon until the mix is well combined.

Spread evenly onto an oven tray lined with parchment paper and bake for roughly 8 minutes or until dark golden brown. Remove from the oven and allow to cool. As the crumble cools down it will become hard and crunchy.

Break the crumble up and store in an airtight container until needed.

For The Goat's Curd

Beat the lemon juice and icing sugar in a medium-sized bowl until the icing sugar is dissolved. Add the goat's curd and lemon zest and beat gently to combine. Cover with cling film and refrigerate.

For The Berries

Remove the tops of the strawberries, then cut in half, or quarters if large, and place into a large bowl.

In a separate bowl, beat the icing sugar, vinegar and lemon juice until smooth and the icing sugar has dissolved. Pour the sugar mix into the strawberries and stir gently until all the strawberries are coated. Add the raspberries to the bowl and stir very gently to combine. Leave the bowl in a warm place to *macerate* for 10 minutes, stirring occasionally.

To Assemble

Preheat the oven to 170°C.

Pour the *macerated* fruit and the juices into a deep oven tray and bake for 5 minutes or until the fruit starts to break down.

Spoon the fruit evenly into 4 bowls, cover with the crumble and a generous dollop of the sweet goat's curd.

146
MARK GREENAWAY

www.markgreenaway.com Twitter: @markgreenaway Facebook: markgreenaway

With a passion for Scottish ingredients, Mark Greenaway uses only the very best local, seasonal produce, transforming it with modern techniques. Mark has been named as one of the top 300 chefs in the world in 2017 and again in 2018; his commitment and drive place him in the very top tier of Scottish chefs.

Mark's career began in Scotland in 1992. He then went on to gain valuable experience during a five year stint in Australia, working at some of the nation's top establishments. On his return to Scotland, Mark continued his profession at One Devonshire Gardens in Glasgow, Kilcamb Lodge Hotel in Strontian and The Dryburgh Abbey Hotel in the Scottish Borders before opening his eponymous restaurant in Edinburgh in 2012. He has since gone on to promote Scottish produce all over the world.

Year on year sees Mark winning awards for his culinary expertise, including winning Best Cookbook in the World in the Chef Category 2017 from the Gourmand Book Awards for his Perceptions cookbook. Perceptions is a feast for the eyes and gives an insight into the workings behind creating many of Mark's stunning dishes, always presented with such innovation.

Photography by Paul Johnston - Copper Mango

The essence of Mark Greenaway's genius in the kitchen is the seemingly endless inventiveness.

MACKEREL, HIBISCUS, APPLE

SERVES 4

 Clemens Strobl 'Donau' Grüner Veltliner Wagram (Austria)

Ingredients

4 mackerel fillets (deboned)

Hibiscus And Elderflower Pickled Shallots

4 shallots (peeled)
60ml elderflower cordial
90ml hibiscus syrup
100ml vegetable stock
25ml cider vinegar
4 coriander seeds
1 star anise

Candied Gooseberries

12 gooseberries
100g caster sugar
50ml water

Beetroot Cured Apple

500ml beetroot juice
100g caster sugar
¼ lemon (juice of)
1 Granny Smith apple

Israeli Couscous

150g Israeli couscous
400ml vegetable stock
1 sprig dill
sea salt (pinch of)

To Serve

16 sprigs affilla cress or pea shoots
edible flower petals

Method

For The Hibiscus And Elderflower Pickled Shallots

Peel the shallots into separate layers and set aside. This is done best by cutting each shallot into quarters, using a small knife to tease the layers apart.

Add the elderflower cordial, hibiscus syrup, stock, vinegar, coriander seeds and star anise to a heavy-based pot and bring to the boil. Pour the boiling liquid over the shallots and set aside until cool. Drain the cooled shallots and reserve the pickling *liquor*.

For The Candied Gooseberries (Prepare ahead)

Gently combine the gooseberries, sugar and water. Vacuum pack and cook at 48°C for 3 hours in a water bath. Alternatively, combine the sugar and water, bring to a rapid boil. Pour over the gooseberries, cling film tightly and store in a warm place for 2-3 hours.

For The Beetroot Cured Apple (Prepare ahead)

Reduce the beetroot juice and sugar down to 200ml, add the lemon juice, then leave to cool.

Using a large Parisienne scoop, scoop out the apple leaving the skin on. Allow 3 per portion.

Drop the apple balls into the beetroot juice, then leave them to infuse for a minimum of an hour.

For The Israeli Couscous

Simmer the couscous in the stock with the dill for 6-8 minutes until tender.

Drain the liquid off and season with salt before setting aside to cool.

For The Mackerel

Blow torch the skin-sides of the mackerel fillets until blackened. This will add great flavour and also cook the fish.

To Finish And Serve

Sprinkle some of the Israeli couscous over each plate, then arrange a mackerel fillet in the centre. Scatter around the pickled shallots, beetroot cured apple, gooseberries, cress or pea shoots and edible petals.

To finish, drizzle over some of the reserved pickling *liquor* from the shallots.

PARTRIDGE, PURPLE SPROUTING BROCCOLI, PEAR

SERVES 4

 Christophe Pacalet's Saint-Amour, Beaujolais (France)

Ingredients

Black Onion Ash

5 onions (cut into thick slices, skin removed)
smoked sea salt

Salt Dough

250g plain flour
3 egg whites
150g rock salt, 75ml water

Salt Baked Pear

3 pears (stalks removed)
salt dough

Broccoli Purée

30g butter
2 shallots (finely diced)
100ml chicken stock
200ml whole milk, 50ml double cream
2 heads broccoli (stalks removed)
100g baby spinach
sea salt

Partridge

4 partridges
rapeseed oil (drizzle of), 50g butter
1 clove garlic (crushed)
1 sprig thyme

Partridge Trimming Jus

reserved bones from the partridges
400ml red wine
6 juniper berries (crushed)
1 litre chicken stock

Purple Sprouting Broccoli

12 spears purple sprouting broccoli (leaves
removed and reserved)
30g butter (melted)
1 tbsp sesame seeds
vegetable oil (for deep frying)
sea salt

Method

For The Black Onion Ash (Prepare ahead)

Season the onions with the salt. Blacken all over in a non-stick pan over a medium heat, turning every 3 or 4 minutes; about 30 minutes as the onions need to be black. Separate the onion layers and dehydrate on full power for 24 hours, or in a low oven. Blend in a food processor, then pass through a fine *chinois*.

For The Salt Dough

Mix the flour, egg whites and rock salt in a mixer for 4 minutes. Slowly add in the water until it becomes a tight dough. Keep mixing for a further 10 minutes.

For The Salt Baked Pear

Preheat the oven to 180°C.
Roll out the salt dough as thinly as possible. Wrap each pear in dough, making sure there are no air bubbles or rips. Bake for 25 minutes. Remove from the oven and crack open the dough. Cool. Using a pastry knife, top and tail the pears and remove the skin. Cut each pear into 4 and dice into ½cm cubes. Store in the fridge.

For The Broccoli Purée

Melt the butter in a heavy-based pan and sweat the shallots over a medium heat with no colour. Add the stock and reduce by half. Pour in the milk and cream and cook for 6-7 minutes. Add the broccoli and spinach and cook for 2 minutes. Drain the liquid from the broccoli and spinach and set aside.
Blend the broccoli and spinach on a high speed, adding a little of the liquid at a time to achieve a thick, glossy purée, then pass through a fine *chinois*. Season with a little salt. Keep warm.

For The Partridge

Preheat the oven to 190°C.
Brown the partridges on all sides in a large pan with a drizzle of rapeseed oil. Transfer the pan to the oven and roast for 9 minutes. Remove from the oven and add the butter, garlic and thyme. Baste, then rest for 6 minutes. Remove the legs and breasts and keep warm. Reserve the bones for the jus.

For The Partridge Trimming Jus

Brown the bones in a heavy-based pan. Add the red wine and juniper berries, then reduce until almost evaporated. Pour in the chicken stock and reduce until there are 200ml left in the pan. Pass through a fine *chinois*. Serve separately.

For The Purple Sprouting Broccoli

Blanch the broccoli in boiling, salted water for 1½ minutes. Drain and toss through the melted butter and some of the sesame seeds. Deep fry the leaves at 185°C. Drain on absorbent paper and season with salt and a sprinkle of sesame seeds.

To Serve

Sprinkle the onion ash all over each plate and serve as pictured.

BROWN BREAD, ORANGE, FIG

SERVES 6

 *Domaine Papagiannakos Melias
(Greece)*

Ingredients

Burnt Orange Jelly

140g caster sugar
1 lime (zest of)
1 lemon (zest of)
1 orange (zest of)
2 vanilla pods (seeds of)
500ml freshly squeezed orange juice
7 leaves gelatine (soaked in cold water)

Brown Bread Parfait

450g brown sourdough (sliced, pulled into chunks)
120g light brown muscovado sugar
1 tsp cinnamon
½ tsp ground ginger
7 egg yolks
325g caster sugar
1½ tbsp liquid glucose
3 egg whites
3 leaves gelatine (soaked in cold water)
750ml double cream (whipped to soft peaks)

Fig Purée

200g caster sugar
300g figs (trimmed, quartered)

Pistachio Powder

60g pistachios (shelled, peeled)
10g caster sugar
5ml pistachio oil

To Serve

chocolate glass swirls (optional)

20cm square tray (lined with cling film)
4cm hemisphere moulds

Method

For The Burnt Orange Jelly

Make a golden caramel with the sugar in a heavy-based pan. Remove from the heat, add the zests and vanilla seeds. Very slowly add the orange juice, stirring frequently. Bring to the boil, add the gelatine and stir until dissolved. Pour through a fine sieve into the prepared tray and leave to cool. When set, cut out circles using a cookie cutter. Keep in the fridge.

For The Brown Bread Parfait

Preheat the oven to 175°C.

Mix the bread with the sugar and spices. Bake in the oven for 20 minutes, turning the bread every 3 minutes until well toasted. Break into rough breadcrumbs and return to the oven for 6 minutes. Leave to cool.

Whisk the egg yolks until pale. Boil 210g of the sugar with the glucose until 118°C, then pour over the yolks. Stir in the gelatine and whisk until cold.

Whisk the egg whites and remaining sugar to make a meringue. Fold all the wet ingredients together, finally fold in the breadcrumbs. Pour into moulds and freeze until firm. Join 2 hemispheres together to make the spheres, freeze until required.

For the Fig Purée

Make a dry caramel with the sugar. Drop the figs into the golden caramel and cook until the water has come out of the figs and evaporated. Blend to a smooth purée, then pass through a fine sieve. Store in the fridge.

For The Pistachio Powder

Preheat the oven to 180°C.

Blend the nuts and sugar to a fine powder. Spread the powder onto a non-stick mat and drizzle with the oil. Bake for 5-6 minutes, then cool. Store in an airtight container.

To Serve

Serve as pictured.

Chef's Tip

Make all elements of this dish in advance for an easy dinner party dessert.

156
MHOR 84 MOTEL

Kings House A84, Balquhidder, Lochearnhead, Perthshire, FK19 8NY

01877 384 646
www.mhor.net Twitter: @mhor84 Facebook: Mhor84 Instagram: Mhor 84 Motel

Surrounded by some of Scotland's most stunning natural scenery, Mhor 84 serves food all day for motel guests, walkers, cyclists, the odd pet dog and everyone else too.

There's always something good to eat at Mhor 84 and, when possible, they source their food from their own farm at Monachyle Mhor. Alternatively, they use the best local suppliers to complement their larder and all baked goods come from the Mhor bakery in Callander.

Open all day for breakfast, lunch and dinner, you can expect everything from a hearty breakfast, a stonking bowl of soup, a great steak, gourmet burger and a selection of the finest fish found in Scottish waters.

When the sun is shining, the front terrace is a hive of activity and, every Thursday throughout the year, you can enjoy traditional music from a range of different bands and musicians, as part of Thank Folk it's Thursday.

Mhor 84 is the perfect place for couples and families alike and if you are a solo traveller, you will always find a like-minded soul to have a natter with over a pint of their very own lager.

Mhor 84 has been a safe haven for travellers since the 1700s and continues to be the perfect stop en route to the Highlands. A funky mix of motel, bar, restaurant and tearoom it is located a mere hour from Edinburgh, Glasgow, Perth and Oban.

SHETLAND SALMON, BEETROOT SLAW, HORSERADISH CREME FRAICHE, ROASTED ALMONDS

SERVES 4

*Glengoyne
12-Year-Old*

Ingredients

Salmon
320g salmon (centre cut, skin-on)
½ lemon (juice of)
butter (knob of)

Beetroot Slaw
2 large raw beetroots (peeled, grated)
2 red onions (thinly sliced)
2 tbsp Maldon sea salt
fennel seeds (pinch of, lightly crushed, toasted)
3 tbsp mayonnaise
1 heaped tbsp English mustard
tarragon (handful of, chopped)
2 Braeburn apples (cut into batons)

Horseradish Crème Fraîche
200g Katy Rogers crème fraîche (the best there is!)
50g creamed horseradish
1 lemon (zest of)
salt and pepper (to taste)
1 tbsp dill (chopped)

Roasted Almonds
100g blanched almonds
1 shallot (finely chopped)
2 tbsp sherry vinegar
40ml Summer Harvest rapeseed oil
1 tbsp parsley (chopped)
½ lemon (juice of)

To Serve
wilted spinach

Method

For The Beetroot Slaw

Mix the grated beetroot and onion together. Season with salt. Leave for 10 minutes for the vegetables to soften. Strain through a colander. Rinse for 1 minute, then squeeze off any excess moisture.

Place the mixture into a mixing bowl and combine all the ingredients. Fold through gently and season to taste.

For The Horseradish Crème Fraîche

Mix all the ingredients together then put it in the fridge to firm up for 30 minutes.

For The Roasted Almonds

Roast the almonds until golden brown. Lightly crush them, then mix all of the ingredients together. Season to taste.

For The Salmon

Cut the salmon into 4 pieces and lightly oil the skin-side.

Heat a non-stick pan and place the salmon in, skin-side down. Cook for 1-2 minutes until the skin is golden brown and crispy. Turn the fish over and cook for a further 2 minutes.

Add a knob of butter and a squeeze of ½ lemon. Once the butter starts to foam, baste the salmon for 30 seconds. Rest for 1 minute before plating.

Chef's Tip
Always remember that the fish will continue to cook at the table with the residual heat.

To Serve
Serve as pictured.

GARETH'S BEEF BURGER, CHIPOTLE KETCHUP

SERVES 4

🍷 *Half pint of West Beer with a 15-Year-Old Glengoyne - 'Half and a Half'!*

Ingredients

Gareth's Beef Burger
500g beef mince
1 small red onion (diced)
½ white onion (diced)
few sprigs thyme (chopped)
2 tbsp tomato paste
1 tbsp English mustard
2 cloves garlic (grated)
parsley (handful of, chopped)
1 egg
20g breadcrumbs
salt and pepper
Tabasco (dash of)

Chipotle Ketchup
500g plum vine tomatoes
1 chipotle dried chilli
20g smoked Maldon salt
20g smoked paprika
2 pears (peeled, cored, roughly chopped)
1 large white onion (roughly chopped)
4 cloves garlic (chopped)
175ml cider vinegar
125g light muscovado sugar
50ml Summer Harvest rapeseed oil

Jean's Dark Beer Bread
450g strong white flour
450g wholemeal seeded flour
25g salt
rapeseed oil (splash of)
20g fresh yeast (ask politely at your local bakers!)
1 tsp honey
320ml warm water, 300ml dark beer

To Serve
tomatoes (sliced)
gherkins (sliced)
red cabbage (shredded)
cheese
iceberg lettuce

Method

For Gareth's Beef Burger
Mix all the ingredients together and taste to check seasoning. Divide the mix into 4 even patties and place in the fridge for about 1 hour to firm up.
Preheat the oven to 180°C (fan).
Very lightly oil the burgers on both sides. Add the patties to a medium to hot frying pan and colour on both sides. Transfer to a hot oven for 6 minutes.

> **Chef's Tip**
> Don't overwork the meat.

For The Chipotle Ketchup (Prepare ahead, makes a 500ml jar)
Heat the rapeseed oil in a large pot on a medium heat.
Mix all of the ingredients together, apart from the sugar, and add to the pot.
Gently simmer for 2 hours, stirring occasionally to stop it catching. Take off the heat and blitz until smooth.
Transfer into a clean pot and add the sugar. Simmer for 30 minutes, then leave to cool. Store in the fridge in a sterilised jar.

To Make Jean's Dark Beer Bread
Place the flours into a big bowl, add the salt and rapeseed oil.
Mix 100ml of the warm water with the yeast and honey. As soon as it starts to bubble add it to the flour and mix together. Slowly add the rest of the water and the beer to the flour mix, little by little, until it all comes together as a dough but is still tacky to the touch. You may not need all of the water or you may need a touch more, see how the dough feels.
Remove the dough from the bowl and place on a lightly floured worktop. Knead it for a couple of minutes until it starts to feel slightly elastic. At this point you may need to add a touch more water. Knead the dough to a count of 50. You should be able to stretch the dough.
Cover with a cloth and set aside in a warm place for 40-60 minutes.
Preheat the oven to 200°C.
Take the dough out of the bowl and mould into your desired shape. Leave to prove again in a warm place for another 20 minutes or so.
Bake in the oven for 20-40 minutes, dependent on the size of the loaf or buns.
You know when it's ready if you tap the bottom of the bread and it sounds hollow. Place on a cooling rack.

To Serve
Serve as pictured.

TREACLE TART, CLOTTED CREAM, CANDIED ORANGE

SERVES 4

 Deanston 12-Year-Old

Ingredients

Pastry

125g unsalted butter (softened)
100g icing sugar
250g plain flour (sifted)
50g ground almonds
1 orange (zest of)
salt (pinch of)
2 large eggs (lightly beaten)

Treacle Filling

220g butter
500g golden syrup
175g treacle
180g wholemeal sourdough breadcrumbs
75ml double cream
2 eggs
1 egg yolk
salt (pinch of)

Candied Orange Peel

1 orange
500ml stock syrup
200g caster sugar

To Serve

clotted cream

Method

For The Pastry

Cream together the butter and sugar. Fold in the flour, ground almonds and salt. Add the eggs to form a dough. Wrap in cling film and rest in the fridge for about an hour or more.

Preheat the oven to 160°C (fan).

Roll the pastry out to 3mm thick. Line the pastry case and blind bake for 30 minutes. Remove the baking beans and cook for a further 10 minutes, until the pastry is crisp and golden.

For The Treacle Filling

Melt the butter over a medium heat until it turns golden brown. Mix in the golden syrup and treacle, then remove from the heat. Pass the mixture through a sieve to remove any solids, then set aside.

Mix the sourdough crumbs in a bowl with the butter and treacle mix. Whisk all the other ingredients in and leave to cool for 15 minutes. Pour into the tart case and cook for a further 40 minutes at 140°C (fan). Serve at room temperature.

For The Candied Orange Peel

Peel the orange and remove any pith. Shred the peel finely and add to the stock syrup. Simmer for 30 minutes, then strain and toss in the caster sugar while still warm.

To Serve

Serve as pictured.

Chef's Tip

This is a favourite of all the staff at Mhor. Don't be tempted to nibble on it before you serve it - or there may be none left!

166
MONACHYLE MHOR HOTEL

Balquhidder, Lochearnhead, Perthshire, FK19 8PQ

01877 384 622 www.monachylemhor.net
Twitter: @MhorHotel Facebook: Monachyle Mhor Hotel Instagram: themhorcollection

Run by the Lewis family and situated in the Loch Lomond and Trossachs National Park, Monachyle Mhor is a boutique hotel and foodie destination that offers guests the very best of Scotland's food and drink, scenery and a warm welcome.

The original jewel in the crown of the Mhor Collection, Monachyle Mhor continues to be a working farm, providing a fine dining experience based on locally sourced, seasonal produce, to visitors from across Scotland, the UK and indeed the world. The ever-changing menu is complemented by an extensive wine list, plethora of whiskies and their very own gins.

With breathtaking views from every direction, across two lochs and some of Scotland's most iconic mountains, this stylish venue offers the perfect setting for the most relaxing of stays, whatever the weather and whatever your taste.

The restaurant itself, housed in a glass fronted conservatory, offers unspoiled views across the front terrace and Loch Voil to the mountains beyond. Featuring 16 rooms and two very unique self-catering properties, Monachyle Mhor blends old and new and brings the building's 16th Century features into the 21st Century.

Monachyle Mhor is four miles off the A84, down a beautiful, peaceful, single-track lane that winds along the wooded banks of Loch Voil.

HAND-DIVED MULL SCALLOP, DRESSED CRAB, GARDEN LEEK

SERVES 4

 Glengoyne 12-Year-Old

Ingredients

Hand-Dived Mull Scallops

4 hand-dived Mull scallops
2 tbsp olive oil
1 tbsp lemon juice
salt and pepper
butter (knob of)

Dressed Crab

2 crabs (picked white crab meat)
1 shallot (finely chopped)
1 tbsp tarragon (finely chopped)
2 tbsp parsley (finely chopped)
½ Granny Smith apple (finely diced)
1 tsp Dijon mustard
1 lemon (juice of)
½ lemon (zest of)
2 tbsp Katy Rogers crème fraîche
salt and pepper (to taste)

Garden Leeks

4 baby garden leeks
100g fresh garden peas (shelled)
salt and pepper (to taste)
vinaigrette (splash of)

Chilli, Ginger And Coriander Dressing

1 red chilli (deseeded, finely chopped)
½ banana shallot (finely chopped)
1cm fresh ginger (peeled, finely chopped)
2 tbsp coriander (finely chopped)
1 lime (juice of)
3-4 tbsp rapeseed oil
salt and pepper (to taste)

Garnish

coriander leaves

Method

For The Chilli, Ginger And Coriander Dressing

Mix all ingredients together and season well.

For The Hand-Dived Mull Scallops

Season the scallops well with salt and pepper. Place them in a pan and cook for 2 minutes, until starting to turn golden. Turn them over, squeeze over the lemon juice and add a knob of butter.

Cook for another minute.

> **Chef's Tip**
> Always use hand-dived scallops.

For The Dressed Crab

Put all ingredients in mixing bowl and fold together. Season with salt and pepper to taste. Place in the fridge until you're ready to serve.

For The Garden Leeks

Blanch the leeks and peas in boiling water. Place in a pan with a splash of vinaigrette. Season well, and wilt for another 30 seconds.

To Serve

Serve as pictured, garnished with fresh coriander leaf.

MONACHYLE VENISON, GARDEN CHARD, BALQUHIDDER CHANTERELLES

SERVES 4

Glengoyne 15-Year-Old
The sweetness of the venison and the earthiness of
the chanterelles makes it the perfect combination.

Ingredients

Venison

1-1½kg venison haunch (seam trimmed)
butter (knob of)
salt and pepper

Roast Shallot And Garlic Purée

3 cloves garlic (unpeeled)
1 sprig thyme
12 whole shallots (unpeeled)
2 tsp sea salt flakes
1 tsp freshly ground black pepper
2 tbsp olive oil
50ml double cream

Garden Vegetables

4-6 rainbow pink chard leaves (washed)
2-4 runner beans (washed, cut evenly)
4-6 carrots (peeled, halved)
4-6 turnips (peeled, halved)
butter (knob of)
salt and pepper

Balquhidder Chanterelles

150g chanterelles
butter (knob of)
salt and pepper
1 tbsp parsley (chopped)
3 leaves tarragon
1 sprig parsley
½ lemon (squeeze of)

Method

For The Venison Haunch

Preheat the oven to 210°C (fan).

Season the venison well.

Heat a frying pan, add the knob of butter and pan fry the venison quickly, until coloured on all sides.

Place the venison in the oven for 4-7 minutes, depending on the size. Remove and transfer to a warm plate to rest for 5 minutes. Reduce the juices in the pan to make a *jus*.

> **Chef's Tip**
>
> Use the freshest venison from Scotland to get the best flavour.

For The Roast Shallot And Garlic Purée

Preheat oven to 180°C (fan).

Place the garlic, thyme and shallots in a small baking dish. Sprinkle with salt, pepper and olive oil, cover with foil and bake until soft, for about 30 minutes. Leave to cool to room temperature.

Peel the garlic and shallots, then purée in a food processor with the double cream. Keep hot.

For The Garden Vegetables

Blanch the carrots, runner beans and turnips in boiling salted water until tender, but still crunchy. Place in iced water to refresh.

Warm a pan, on a medium heat, and melt the butter. Add the *blanched* garden vegetables and chard leaves. Wilt for a minute, season well with salt and pepper. Serve immediately.

For The Balquhidder Chanterelles

Clean the mushrooms with a pastry brush. Heat a pan on a medium to hot heat, add a knob of butter, then the chanterelles. Season with salt and pepper. Add the chopped parsley and tarragon.

Spritz with a squeeze of lemon juice.

To Serve

Serve as pictured.

WARM BRAMBLES, BROWN BREAD ICE CREAM, HEATHER HONEY SOURDOUGH CRISP

SERVES 8

 Glengoyne 18-Year-Old

Ingredients

Brown Bread Ice Cream

1 loaf brown bread
6 tsp ground cinnamon
8 tbsp Demerara sugar
500ml whole milk
500ml double cream
1 vanilla pod (split in half, scraped)
2 tbsp heather honey
12 egg yolks
150g caster sugar
1-2 lemons (juice of, to taste)

Heather Honey Sourdough Crisp

¼ sourdough loaf (partially frozen)
2 tbsp heather honey

Warm Brambles

400g brambles
1 tbsp heather honey
lemon juice (squeeze of)
1 tsp sugar

Method

For The Brown Bread Ice Cream (Prepare ahead)

Preheat the oven to 180°C (fan).

Crumble half the loaf of bread. Mix with half the cinnamon and 5 tablespoons of Demerara. Toast in the oven for 15 minutes. Pour the milk and cream over the toasted bread and leave for 1 hour to infuse.

Strain the mixture, add the heather honey and vanilla and bring gradually to the boil.

Whisk the egg yolks and caster sugar until pale white. Pour a little of the heated cream into the egg yolks, then pour back into the pan. Whisk constantly until the mixture coats the back of the spoon. Leave to cool.

Remove the middle/soft part from the other half of the bread and place in the blender. Blitz with the rest of the cinnamon and sugar until it reaches a fine crumb. Place in the oven for 15-20 minutes until crispy and golden in colour. Add the lemon juice to your taste, to the ice cream base. Churn in an ice cream machine until the ice cream becomes soft in texture, then add the brown breadcrumbs and finish churning the ice cream. Place in the freezer.

For The Heather Honey Sourdough Crisp

Preheat oven to 200°C (fan).

Thinly slice the sourdough loaf and place on a flat baking tray with a silicone mat. Using a pastry brush, paint the honey all over the sourdough slices. Bake in the oven for 10-15 minutes until golden brown.

Remove from the tray and place on a cooling rack.

For The Warm Brambles

Preheat oven to 200°C (fan).

Put everything into a pan and place into the oven for 5 minutes. Finish the brambles with a splash of your favourite malt whisky when they come out of the oven.

> **Chef's Tip**
>
> Don't overcook the brambles. Warm them through, don't cook them.

To Serve

Serve as pictured.

176
THE OYSTERCATCHER

Otter Ferry, Tighnabruaich, Argyll, PA21 2DH

01700 821 229
www.theoystercatcher.co.uk Facebook: The Oystercatcher - Otter Ferry Instagram: _oystercatcher

Originally the ferry-man's house, and sitting just 20 metres from the banks of Loch Fyne, The Oystercatcher in Otter Ferry is the first (and last!) joint venture for husband and wife team Chloe Stapleton and David Wall. If you are brave enough to take either of the three single track roads that lead to The Oystercatcher, you are immediately rewarded with undisturbed views of Loch Fyne and the Kintyre Peninsula.

On a sunny day, there is nowhere better to eat fresh Tarbert shellfish, or enjoy slow braised rare breed Auchinbreck pork. The lamb comes from the hills at Shellfield farm, a mere three miles away, whilst the oysters are farmed on the estate. All this matched with craft beers sourced locally and from all around Scotland, 16 different small batch gins and a hand-picked single malt whisky selection.

The Oystercatcher, Otter Ferry is the combined effort of a small, dedicated team and committed suppliers who care about the service, food, drink and produce they provide.

"We hope our food and our service reflect the way we like to eat. Our menu changes seasonally but our stunning setting and welcoming atmosphere remain a constant throughout the year." Chloe Stapleton and David Wall.

WELCOME TO
THE OYSTERCATCHER

OTTER FERRY

CURED GRAVLAX, TREACLE & PUMPKIN SEED RYE, BEETROOT RELISH, YOGHURT

SERVES 4

 Spicy Bloody Mary

Ingredients

Gravlax
½ side responsibly sourced salmon
250-300g sea salt
250-300g caster sugar
35ml of your favourite single malt whisky
1 tbsp Dijon mustard
dill (bunch of, chopped)

Yoghurt
500ml double cream
500ml whole milk
250ml live yoghurt

Pumpkin Seed Rye Bread
250g rye flour
250g strong white flour (plus extra for dusting)
15g Maldon sea salt
15g caster sugar
15g dry yeast
pumpkin seeds (handful of)
50g treacle
50g yoghurt
500ml warm water

Beetroot Relish
2 good sized beetroots
50g dark brown muscovado sugar
50ml red wine vinegar

Garnish
wild garlic flowers

banneton basket
pizza stone

Method

For The Gravlax (Allow 48 hours)

Score the salmon skin 3-4 times. Mix the salt and sugar together in a bowl and place half the mix in a plastic tray large enough to fit the salmon. Place the salmon, skin-side down, in the tray and cover with the remaining sugar/salt mix. Cover the tray and refrigerate for 24 hours.

Remove the salmon from the fridge and wash with cold water. Pat dry, then massage the whisky into the salmon. Cover the flesh with the mustard and dill. Cling film the salmon and refrigerate for another 24 hours before slicing thinly to serve.

Chef's Tip

Be careful not to overcure the salmon and always leave to rest for a day before eating.

For The Yoghurt (Prepare ahead)

Place the cream and milk in a heavy-based saucepan. Bring up to 83°C to pasteurise. Allow to cool to 43°C, then whisk in the yoghurt. Cover with cling film and leave in a warm room to set for 12 hours.

For The Pumpkin Seed Rye Bread

Mix all the dry ingredients in a large bowl and all the wet ingredients in a separate bowl before combining them. Knead for 2-3 minutes until a smooth, velvety dough is formed. Prove in a warm place for 3-4 hours before kneading again.

Preheat the oven to 250°C.

Flour the dough and place in a floured banneton basket and prove again for another hour before tipping the dough out onto a pizza stone. Bake in the oven for 30-40 minutes. Leave to cool before slicing.

For The Beetroot Relish

Boil the beetroots in salted water until cooked. Transfer the beets to a jug blender, add the sugar and vinegar and blitz until smooth.

To Serve

Serve as pictured.

BOUILLABAISSE WITH HAKE & LOCAL SHELLFISH

SERVES 4

🍷 *A chilled glass of 2016 Cuvée Caroline Morin Picpoul De Pinet (France)*

Ingredients

Bouillabaisse

1 large, Spanish white onion (roughly diced)
1 bulb garlic (roughly diced)
1 tbsp oil
10 tomatoes (roughly chopped)
2 carrots (roughly chopped)
2 sticks celery (roughly chopped)
2 heads fresh fennel (roughly chopped)
2 litres fish stock
2 tbsp fennel seeds
2 tbsp pink peppercorns
1 tbsp hot chilli powder
1 orange (peeled rind of)
50ml Cointreau
2 hake fillets (cut into chunks)
1kg shellfish of your choosing (mussels, clams, crayfish etc)

Garnish

fresh dill
pink peppercorns
fennel fronds
wild garlic flowers

Method

For The Bouillabaisse

Brown the onion and garlic in the oil in a large pan. Add the tomatoes, carrots, celery and fennel and cook until softened.

Pour in the fish stock and add the fennel seeds, peppercorns and chilli powder. Cook for 1 hour. Using a stick blender, blend as smooth as possible before passing through a sieve. Discard the pulp, then add the orange peel and Cointreau to the smooth *liquor*.

To Serve

Add the fish and shellfish and bring to the boil to cook the fish. Garnish with fresh dill, pink peppercorns and fennel fronds.

> **Chef's Tip**
> Use 'skin-on' fish fillets to prevent the fish breaking up when cooking.

PORTUGUESE CUSTARD TARTS, RHUBARB SORBET, CRUSHED PISTACHIOS

SERVES 6

 A double espresso

Ingredients

Rough Puff Pastry

250g plain flour (plus extra for rolling)
sea salt (pinch of)
180ml water
250g butter (room temperature)

Custard

250g caster sugar
1 stick cinnamon
½ lemon (peel of)
250ml water
25g plain flour
12g cornflour
300ml whole milk
4 free-range egg yolks
1 free-range egg
vanilla essence (dash of)

Rhubarb Sorbet

500g rhubarb (cut into small chunks)
500g caster sugar
water (splash of)
1 lime (juice of)

Garnish

pistachios (crushed)
12 rhubarb batons (poached)

muffin tin

Method

For The Rough Puff Pastry

Place the flour, salt and water in a bowl and mix together until a soft, pillowy dough forms. Rest for 10 minutes before rolling the dough on a heavily floured surface to form a 30cm square. Spread a quarter of the butter over the dough before folding the dough. Spread the folded dough with the remaining butter and roll into a tight log. Refrigerate for at least 2 hours until the dough is firm.

Chef's Tip

The pastry can be quite sticky so be generous with the flour!

For The Custard

Make a stock syrup by bringing the sugar, cinnamon, lemon peel and water to the boil. Reduce the heat and simmer for 3 minutes. Leave to cool, then remove the lemon peel and cinnamon stick.

Combine the flours in a bowl with a splash of milk and stir until a paste is formed. Place the remaining milk in a pan and bring to the boil before gradually adding the flour mix until smooth. Slowly add the sugar syrup and whisk in the egg, egg yolks and vanilla. Set aside.

To Assemble And Bake The Portuguese Tarts

Preheat the oven to 250°C.

Remove the pastry log from the fridge and let soften slightly. Slice the log into 2½cm discs and place in a well greased muffin tin. With a buttery thumb, work the pastry up the sides of the muffin tin to form pastry cups. Pour the custard mix into the pastry cups until three-quarters full. Bake for 10-12 minutes or until the custard is set with a slight wobble.

For The Rhubarb Sorbet

Place the rhubarb and sugar in a pan with a splash of water. Simmer until the rhubarb is soft, then strain the juice and squeeze in the lime. Churn in an ice cream machine, then freeze until set.

To Serve

Serve as pictured with crushed pistachios.

186
THE PEAT INN

Peat Inn, by St Andrews, Fife, KY15 5LH

01334 840 206
www.thepeatinn.co.uk Twitter: @thepeatinn Facebook: @thepeatinn

The Peat Inn is a Michelin starred restaurant near St Andrews owned and run since 2006 by chef Geoffrey Smeddle and his wife Katherine. Built around 1750 as a coaching inn near a well-known local area for peat, a village soon grew up around the inn. The building became known among locals as The Peat Inn, after the local fuel that was dug there, with the village taking the same name over time. Centuries later, the address remains The Peat Inn, Peat Inn.

Today The Peat Inn is a celebrated restaurant with rooms, using Scottish ingredients with sympathy, simplicity and skill. The resulting cuisine is grounded in classical techniques with some subtle contemporary touches, but always offers guests dishes which are designed to bring comfort and pleasure. The restaurant has been awarded a star in the Michelin guide every year since 2010 and also features in the Good Food Guide top 50 UK restaurants. There are eight beautifully appointed suites too, allowing guests to truly relax and appreciate this cherished destination.

A contemporary Michelin starred restaurant with roots dating back to the 18th Century.

THE PEAT INN
RESTAURANT

THE
PEAT
INN

ROAST HAKE WRAPPED IN PANCETTA, PARSLEY PUREE, FRESH PEAS, MORELS, SEA KALE

SERVES 4

 Capellania, Marques de Murrieta, White Rioja Reserva 2011 (Spain)

Ingredients

Hake

4 x 80-90g pieces of hake (skinned, trimmed)
12 rashers thinly sliced pancetta

Parsley Purée

2 bunches curly parsley (leafy part picked)
baby spinach (handful of)
100ml double cream

Morels

60g unsalted butter
1 banana shallot (finely diced)
8 fresh morels (well washed, sliced into quarters)
150ml Madeira
200ml brown chicken jus

Garnish

fresh peas
8 small stems sea kale
pea shoots or other soft herb of your choice,
such as chervil sprigs

Method

For The Hake

Lay out 4 slices of pancetta so they overlap along the long length of the meat. Place 1 piece of fish across, then roll over until it is completely wrapped. Trim any excess pancetta at each end so it is a neat parcel. Set aside and repeat with the remaining pancetta and fish until all 4 are wrapped.

For The Parsley Purée

Blanch the spinach and parsley in rapidly boiling, salted water for 2 minutes, then refresh in ice cold water. Drain and squeeze out the water carefully. Heat the cream in a small saucepan. Combine the cream and the blanched parsley mixture. Blitz in a powerful blender to a silky, smooth purée.

For The Morels

Melt the butter in a small saucepan and sweat the shallots slowly with a little salt until soft, without colouring, about 10 minutes. Add the morels, stir in well and fry for a further 3 minutes. Add the Madeira and reduce by half. Pour in the chicken jus and simmer for 5 minutes or until the liquid has slightly thickened to a sauce consistency. Set aside.

> **Chef's Tip**
>
> Dried morels are one of the rare ingredients that can be substituted for the fresh original product and still work as well if fresh are not available.

To Serve

Preheat the oven to 180°C.

Heat a non-stick pan, add a film of olive oil and, after 1 minute, add the fish. Carefully brown on all sides, then transfer to the oven for 4 minutes. Heat the morels in the chicken jus. Boil the peas for 3 minutes and the sea kale for 1 minute, drain, season lightly. Place a spoonful of warmed parsley purée on the serving plate. Cut each piece of fish in half and arrange 2 pieces attractively on each plate. Scatter the peas over and around the fish. Lay the kale over the fish. Finally, spoon the morels and their sauce around the dish. Arrange the pea shoots or soft herbs on the plate and serve at once.

FILLETS OF JOHN DORY, RAZOR CLAMS, POACHED ONIONS, WILD HERBS, VERMOUTH VELOUTE

SERVES 4

🍷 *Premier Cru Les Frionnes, Saint-Aubin Hubert Lamy 2014 (France)*

Ingredients

Poached Onions

10ml olive oil, 40g unsalted butter
2 medium sized onions (peeled, sliced into rounds ½cm thick, seasoned with salt)
100ml white wine, 300ml vegetable stock

Vermouth Velouté

2 large banana shallots (peeled, finely sliced)
10 whole white peppercorns, 10 fennel seeds, 1 star anise
thyme (few bushy sprigs of)
tarragon (several stems of)
salt (pinch of)
150ml white wine, 150ml vermouth
500ml fish stock, 200ml double cream
1 lemon (zest and juice of)

Razor Clams

2 sticks celery (leaves reserved, 1 finely sliced, 1 sliced 3mm thick)
1 small shallot (sliced)
thyme (few sprigs of), parsley and tarragon stalks
40g unsalted butter
8 fresh razor clams (soaked in cold water for 2 hours, then drained)
150ml white wine

John Dory, Wild Herbs, Mushrooms

320g wild herb leaves (alexanders, wild leeks, wild garlic, wood sorrel)
1 clove garlic (peeled)
50g unsalted cold butter (diced)
8 John Dory fillets or white fish of choice (seasoned with salt)
oil (a drizzle of)
1 lemon (cut into wedges)
100g scarlet elf caps wild mushrooms or sliced chestnut mushrooms (*sautéed* in foaming butter)

Method

For The Poached Onions

Preheat the oven to 160°C.

Warm a large frying pan, melt the butter and oil. Add the onions ensuring they stay intact. Cook on low for 5 minutes, add the wine and reduce by half. Add the stock, bring to a simmer, cover with a *cartouche*, bake for 30 minutes. Drain on a cloth.

For The Vermouth Velouté

Sweat the shallots, spices, herbs and salt until soft without colouring, add the wine and vermouth. Boil, reduce by half, add the stock, reduce by a third, then add the cream. Bring to a simmer, add the lemon zest and juice, then cover with cling film. Set aside for 30 minutes. Strain through a fine sieve into a clean pan.

For The Razor Clams

Sweat the finely sliced celery, shallot and herbs in 30g of butter until soft without colouring. Increase the heat, add the clams and wine and reduce by half. Cover with a lid, cook for 5 minutes or until the clams are fully open. Lift the clams out onto a clean tray to cool, then strain the *liquor* into a small pan.

Remove the meat and reserve the shells. Slice the firm, meaty finger of clam flesh into rounds, discard the frill and other sections. Rinse the shells and reserve the 4 best. Soften the celery slices in a little butter, then mix with the clams, reserved clam juice and celery leaf. Reserve in the clam shells.

For The John Dory, Wild Herbs, Mushrooms And To Serve

Wilt the herbs in 20g of butter with the garlic, then drain. Discard the garlic. Arrange 2 onion pieces and the herbs on each plate. Warm the filled clams in a moderate oven. Heat a large non-stick frying pan for 1 minute, add a light film of oil and heat for a further minute. Sear the fish until golden in the hot oil, about 2 minutes. Add 30g of butter, flip the fish over. Baste rapidly, then lift the fish out onto a clean tray lined with paper towel. Spritz with lemon, then spoon the pan juices over the fish. Plate the fish and warmed clams, scatter the mushrooms. Hand blend the hot sauce and spoon over the plate. Serve at once.

Chef's Tip

You can replace the wild herbs with a mix of wilted spinach and little gem leaves.

PRALINE MOUSSE, DARK CHOCOLATE CREMEUX, SALTED CARAMEL SAUCE

SERVES 8

 Rivesaltes Ambré Domaine Fontanel 2007 (France)

Ingredients

Praline Mousse

30g egg white
30g caster sugar
90ml double cream
2 leaves gelatine (softened in ice cold water)
75g praline paste

Chocolate Crémeux

125ml whole milk
125ml double cream
50g caster sugar
60g egg yolk
80g good quality dark chocolate (70%)

Salted Caramel Sauce

175ml double cream
1 vanilla pod (split, seeds scraped out)
125g caster sugar
8g Maldon sea salt flakes

Financier Base

10g dark chocolate (70%)
110g butter (to foaming nut brown butter stage)
125g icing sugar
10g cocoa powder
40g plain flour
120g egg white
60g ground almonds

To Serve

crème fraîche
dark chocolate shavings
caramelised or toasted hazelnuts

8 x 7cm diameter moulds

Method

For The Praline Mousse (Prepare ahead)

Whisk the egg white and sugar to stiff peaks. Whip 60ml of double cream to ribbon stage. Heat the remaining cream, squeeze out the excess water from the soaked gelatine and dissolve in the hot cream. Add to the praline paste. Whisk 2 spoons of whisked egg white into the praline mix to loosen it then fold in the rest of the egg white. Combine with the cream. Set in the moulds. Freeze until hard, then remove from the moulds and store in the fridge on greaseproof paper.

For The Chocolate Crémeux

Boil the milk, cream and sugar and pour over the egg yolks. Cook until coating the back of a spoon. Remove from the heat and pour over the chocolate, whisk to *emulsify* and allow to set. Transfer to a piping bag, then chill.

For The Salted Caramel Sauce

Boil the cream with the vanilla pod and seeds. In a separate pan, make a dry caramel with the sugar, then remove the vanilla pod from the cream, rinse and reserve for other uses. Dissolve the salt in the cream, then combine the cream with the caramel, slowly and carefully as it will be extremely hot. Leave to cool. Store in a squeezy bottle at room temperature.

For The Financier Base

Preheat the oven to 180°C.

Melt the chocolate in the hot butter and leave to cool. Sieve all the dry ingredients together. Whisk the egg whites into the dry mixture. Mix the cool butter and chocolate mix into the egg white mixture. Spread a ½cm layer on greaseproof paper and bake for 7-9 minutes until set like a thin, gooey sponge. Cool and cut out discs the same size as the base of the mousse.

> **Chef's Tip**
> The chocolate financier base can be made using gluten free flour.

To Assemble And Serve

Scoop out a small amount of praline mousse from the underside of the dome using a melon baller. Fill with salted caramel sauce, then place a chocolate financier base over it to keep the caramel in place. Carefully place on a tray and pipe the crémeux all over to create hedgehog spikes. Transfer to a serving plate using a spatula. Pipe some dots of caramel sauce on the plate and finish with a scoop of thick crème fraîche. Garnish with dark chocolate shavings and caramelised or toasted hazelnuts and serve at once.

196
PURSLANE RESTAURANT

33a St Stephen Street, Edinburgh, EH3 5AH

0131 226 3500
www.purslanerestaurant.co.uk Twitter: Purslane_1 Instagram Purslane1

Bringing with him a wealth of experience, chef proprietor Paul Gunning has worked in 5 star hotels, 2 and 3 AA Rosette restaurants as well as Michelin starred restaurants, gleaning experience from the likes of Marco Pierre White (Riverroom MPW), Jeff Bland (Balmoral, Number 1), Phil Thompson (Auberge Du Lac) and Jean Michel Gauffre (La Garrigue). Paul is keen to pass on his skills and continue to learn from the small, friendly and loyal team that he has in Purslane.

Diners will experience what Paul calls "casual fine-dining". The restaurant has an unpretentious and casual feel to it with no dress code or formality. "We want customers to feel relaxed at all times," says Paul. "Customers feel free to ask questions about the food or wines without being intimidated. If the diners are happy, the team is happy." And this approach seems to work. Since its inception in 2011, Purslane has built up a regular clientele who return to taste the seasonally dictated menus. "It is important to us to use the freshest of seasonal ingredients to ensure the best quality, sourced as locally as we can. The majority of our suppliers are based within a stone's throw of the restaurant.

We hope that by keeping it local, we help to bring a sense of community to the restaurant as well as helping fellow small businesses."

With a mix of old and new techniques using worldwide influences, Purslane showcases its food in a lunch menu, à la carte or 5 or 7 course tasting menus offered with matching wines if desired. Alternatively, diners can select from the carefully chosen wine list which offers something for every palate and wallet.

PURSLANE

RESTAURANT

"Ambitious modern dishes which mix tried-and-tested flavours with modern techniques." Michelin Guide *****

SCALLOPS, CAULIFLOWER, RAISIN PUREE

SERVES 4

🍷 *Saskia, Chenin Blanc/Viognier/Clairette Blanche,*
Miles Mossop, 2014, (Coastal Region, South Africa)

Ingredients

Cauliflower Purée And Beignets

1 large cauliflower
100g butter
100ml double cream
150ml chicken stock
salt (pinch of)
20ml vegetable oil
50g plain flour
70ml sparkling water
oil (to deep fry)

Raisin Purée And Plumped Raisins

110g raisins
20g capers
50g sugar
50ml Pedro Ximenez sherry

Scallops

8 scallops
oil (drizzle of)
salt (pinch of)

Garnish

micro herbs

Method

For The Cauliflower Purée And Beignets

Remove 16 small cauliflower florets for the beignets and
set aside.

Finely chop the remaining cauliflower and put in a pot with
the butter, cream, chicken stock and salt. Simmer gently for
15 minutes.

Drain the cauliflower, reserving the cooking liquid. Put the
cauliflower in a blender, adding some of the cooking liquid and
blend until it is a smooth consistency. If lumpy, keep adding a
little liquid until the desired consistency is achieved.

Take 8 of the cauliflower florets, season and drizzle with oil.
Colour in a frying pan on a medium heat until coloured all over,
about 5 minutes.

To make the beignet batter, mix the flour and sparkling water.
Dip the remaining florets into the batter, then deep fry (180°C)
for 2 minutes until crispy. Remove onto kitchen roll and season.

Chef's Tip

Use ice cold sparkling water for the batter to create a
crispier finish.

For The Raisin Purée And Plumped Raisins

Put 100g of the raisins and the capers in a pot. Cover with
water and add the sugar. Bring to the boil and cook for 10-15
minutes. Transfer to a blender and blitz until smooth.

Heat the sherry and add the remaining 10g of raisins. Simmer
gently for 10 minutes, then leave to reconstitute and cool in
the sherry.

For The Scallops

Heat a non-stick frying pan. Oil and season the scallops, then
place them in the hot pan. Cook the scallops on one side until
golden brown, 1-1½ minutes depending on the size. Turn over
and cook for a further 1-1½ minutes or until the scallops are
slightly firm to touch.

To Serve

Arrange on the plate as pictured and garnish with micro herbs.

ROAST HALIBUT, SAUTEED LEEKS, CHAMPAGNE & CAVIAR VELOUTE

SERVES 4

 Chablis 1er Cru, Les Lys, Domaine Vincent Dampt, 2015 (France)

Ingredients

Champagne And Caviar Velouté

3 shallots (peeled, sliced)
5 cloves garlic (halved)
10 sprigs thyme
vegetable oil (drizzle of)
100ml Champagne
100ml chicken stock
200ml double cream
salt (pinch of)
10g caviar
chives (chopped)

Onions

100ml white wine vinegar
20g sugar
24 silverskin onions

Potatoes

4 large purple potatoes
oil (drizzle of)
5 cloves garlic (halved)
10 sprigs thyme
salt (pinch of)

Sautéed Leeks

2 leeks
oil (drizzle of)
10g butter

Roast Halibut

4 x 160g halibut fillets
10g butter
1 sprig thyme
1 clove garlic (crushed)
lemon (spritz of)

To Serve

1 cucumber

Method

For The Champagne And Caviar Velouté

Sauté the shallots, halved garlic cloves and thyme in a little oil for a few minutes. Add the Champagne, reduce by half, then add the chicken stock and reduce by half again. Pour in the cream and simmer gently for 5 minutes. Pass through a fine sieve and correct the seasoning.

For The Onions

Boil the vinegar and sugar, then add the onions. Remove from the heat and leave them to pickle.

For The Potatoes

Preheat the oven to 180°C.

Slice the potatoes into 2½cm pieces, then cut out 24 cylinders using a small cutter. Toss the potato cylinders in a bowl with a drizzle of oil, the garlic, thyme and salt. Place on a baking tray, cover with foil and roast for 15 minutes or until the potatoes are cooked.

For The Sautéed Leeks

Remove the outer leaves of the leeks and discard. Wash the leeks, then thinly slice. Add a drizzle of oil to a pan and the butter. Once foaming, add the leeks, season and cook quickly for 2 minutes. Remove from the heat and drain on kitchen roll.

For The Roast Halibut

Heat a non-stick pan. Season and oil the halibut and place in the pan. Cook on one side until golden. Add the butter, thyme and garlic and baste until cooked. Add a spritz of lemon.

> **Chef's Tip**
> Remove the halibut from the fridge 10 minutes before you cook it. This helps bring the fish to room temperature to ensure even cooking.

To Serve

Using a small melon baller, cut 24 balls from the cucumber. Gently heat the Champagne velouté and finish with the caviar and chives. Plate all the ingredients as pictured and spoon the velouté generously over the halibut.

POACHED RHUBARB, VANILLA PANNA COTTA, VANILLA ICE CREAM, RHUBARB CLAFOUTIS

SERVES 4-6

Royal Tokaji, 5 Puttonyos Aszu, 2013
(Hungary)

Ingredients

Vanilla Ice Cream

300ml double cream
300ml whole milk
1 vanilla pod (split)
4 egg yolks
100g caster sugar

Vanilla Panna Cotta

300ml whole milk
300ml double cream
2 vanilla pods (split)
100g caster sugar
1½ leaves gelatine (soaked in cold water)

Rhubarb Clafoutis

50g ground almonds
100g caster sugar
2 large eggs
2 egg yolks
250ml double cream
salt (pinch of)
1 stick rhubarb (cut into 1cm slices)
icing sugar (for dusting)

Poached Rhubarb

4 sticks rhubarb
100ml water
100g sugar

Garnish

mint
biscuit crumb
tuile

4-6 panna cotta moulds
mini muffin silicone mould

Method

For The Vanilla Ice Cream

Heat the cream and milk with the vanilla pod over a low heat, stirring occasionally, until it almost boils. You will see a few bubbles at the edge. Remove from the heat and set aside for 30 minutes to infuse.

Put the egg yolks in a bowl with the sugar and beat until the mixture has thickened, is paler in colour and falls in thick ribbons when you lift the beaters.

Add a little of the warm milk mix to the egg yolks, mix well, then return to the pan with the rest of the milk mix. Cook on a low heat, stirring constantly with a wooden spoon, for 8-10 minutes until it coats the back of a spoon. Cool, then churn in an ice cream machine.

Chef's Tip

When making the ice cream, ensure the mixture does not boil. As soon as you see any bubbles about to burst to the surface, remove from the heat so it doesn't curdle.

For The Vanilla Panna Cotta

Warm the milk, cream, vanilla and sugar, then leave to infuse for 30 minutes. Reheat a little of the milk mix, stir in the soaked gelatine until dissolved, then add to the remaining milk. Pass through a fine sieve. Pour into the moulds and chill for 3 hours.

For The Rhubarb Clafoutis

Preheat the oven to 180°C.

Combine the almonds, caster sugar, eggs, cream and salt, then leave to rest for 30 minutes. Pour into the silicone moulds. Add the rhubarb slices to the mixture in the moulds. Bake for 15-20 minutes. Leave to cool for 30 minutes, then remove from the moulds and dust with icing sugar.

For The Poached Rhubarb

Cut the rhubarb into large batons. Bring the water and sugar to the boil, add the rhubarb, then remove from the heat. Leave the rhubarb for 15 minutes to cool in the syrup, then drain.

To Serve

Turn out the panna cottas using warm water to briefly and gently warm the moulds. Arrange with the remaining elements and garnish as pictured.

206 TORAVAIG HOUSE HOTEL

Knock Bay, Isle of Skye, IV44 8RE

01471 820 200
www.toravaig.com. Twitter: @Toravaig. Facebook: Toravaig House Hotel

Toravaig House on the enchanting Isle of Skye is a small boutique hotel, within a collection of three family-owned hotels on the island known as the Sonas Collection. The collection is owned and run by Anne Gunn whose accolades include Scottish Hotelier of the Year and a Gold Laurel as Scotland's 'most visionary entrepreneur'. The kitchen is led by head chef Miles Craven, Scottish Food Awards 2018 Gold Medal winner for Creative Chef.

Toravaig House is situated in an elevated, south facing position on the south peninsula, enjoying views out across the Atlantic waters of the Sound of Sleat over to the distant hills of Arisaig. Along with many other accolades including 2 AA Rosettes, this Hebridean gem has recently been named 'Scottish Island Hotel of the Year' 2018 at the Scottish Hotel Awards. With its comfortable lounge, open fire and baby grand piano, this is a beautiful place to begin your dining experience after a day exploring the beautiful landscapes.

Guests enjoy an elegant dining experience in Toravaig's Iona restaurant. The kitchen team uses the best of Skye's natural larder from the hills, gardens, rivers and sea, to ensure the dishes are a true taste of the Island.

Having been fully refurbished in 2017, the accommodation in Toravaig House is made up of nine individually designed contemporary bedrooms. Incorporating colours and textures that complement each other beautifully, the fabrics and furnishings offer a muted pallete of browns, creams and mauves to echo the Highland landscape, while being sophisticated and calming. Toravaig makes a wonderful venue where your hosts go that extra mile to ensure your visit is most memorable.

Toravaig
HOUSE

HOTEL & RESTAURANT

IONA
RESTAURANT

Toravaig House on the enchanting Isle of Skye, a small boutique hotel serving the finest cuisine that Skye's legendary larder can provide.

LAMB SWEETBREADS, LANGOUSTINE, BROCCOLI

SERVES 4

 Pouilly Fumé, Patrice Moreux, 2015 (France)

Ingredients

Lamb Sweetbreads

200g lamb sweetbreads
olive oil (glug of)
butter (large knob of)

Langoustines

4 large langoustines
olive oil (glug of)

Broccoli

3 heads broccoli
10ml cream
salt and pepper
200g Tenderstem broccoli

Sauce Américaine

langoustine heads
1 carrot (*brunoise*)
2 shallots (*brunoise*)
1 fennel bulb (diced)
1 plum tomato (*brunoise*)
50ml white wine
50ml brandy
100ml chicken stock
200ml veal stock

Method

For The Lamb Sweetbreads

Rinse the sweetbreads under cold running water, then degorge in heavily salted water for 1 hour. Wash, then put in a pan of water and bring to the boil. Remove from the heat and leave them in the water until cool. Fry until golden brown on all sides in oil, then in foaming butter.

For The Langoustines

Remove the heads, de-vein the langoustines, then peel. Pan fry for a couple of minutes in oil.

Chef's Tip

To easily peel the langoustines, *blanch* in boiling water for 10 seconds, then refresh in ice cold water.

For The Broccoli Purée And Tenderstem Broccoli

Shave the green tips off the broccoli and boil in boiling, salted water for 4 minutes, then strain and blend in a food processor with some of the cooking *liquor*. Finish with a splash of cream and season.

Trim the ends of the Tenderstem broccoli and boil for 3 minutes in seasoned water.

For The Sauce Américaine

Cut the langoustine heads in half and roast in a hot pan. Remove the heads, then add the carrot, shallots, fennel and tomato to the same pan and *sauté* until softened. Pour in the white wine and brandy and reduce by two-thirds. Add the stocks and reduce until it coats the back of a spoon. Pass through a fine *chinois*.

To Serve

Serve as pictured.

DUCK, CARROT, APRICOT, PAN SEARED FOIE GRAS

SERVES 4

 Critèra Primitivo, Schola Sarmenti
(Italy)

Ingredients

2 duck breasts

Duck Brine

100g sea salt flakes
50g Demerara sugar
1 tbsp honey
2 bay leaves
8 peppercorns
4 cloves
750ml water
250ml red wine

Pan Jus

1 glass red wine
50ml chicken stock
butter (knob of)

Carrot Purée

100g dried apricots
50ml light stock syrup (50g sugar/50ml water)
1 bay leaf
1 star anise
1 orange (peel of)
500g carrots
200ml cold pressed rapeseed oil

Heritage Carrots

2 heritage carrots (peeled)
30g butter
30g honey

Savoy Cabbage

1 Savoy cabbage (shredded)
butter (large knob of)

Foie Gras

4 slices foie gras
oil (a drizzle of)

Garnish

12 candied almonds

Method

For The Duck Brine (Prepare ahead)

Mix all the ingredients together in a pan and bring to the boil, ensuring all the sugar and salt has dissolved. Allow to cool.

For The Duck (Prepare ahead)

Place the duck into the cold brine for 45 minutes. Remove from the brine and leave on absorbent paper overnight.

Preheat the oven to 180°C.

Heat a dry pan on a medium high heat, cook the duck skin-side down, gently pressing against the pan to ensure all skin is in contact with the heat. Allow the skin to crisp up and render for 1-2 minutes, then remove from the pan and place skin-side down on a tray in the oven for 4 minutes. Rest skin-side up.

For The Pan Jus

Bring the wine and stock to the boil in the pan used to cook the duck in and allow to reduce by half. Stir in the butter to *emulsify* just before serving.

For The Carrot Purée (Prepare ahead)

Soak the apricots in a light stock syrup with the bay leaf, orange peel and star anise and leave overnight. Grate the carrots and cook in rapeseed oil until soft. Blend in a food processor with the soaked apricots.

> **Chef's Tip**
> Don't use oil when cooking the duck as fat from the duck itself will render and ensure crispy skin.

For The Heritage Carrots

Preheat the oven to 180°C (fan).

Roast the carrots on a tray with the honey and butter until golden and caramelised.

For The Savoy Cabbage

Sauté with no colour until soft, then stir in the butter.

For The Foie Gras

Gently pan fry the foie gras in a little oil.

To Serve

Assemble all the elements as pictured.

WHISKY SET CREAM, PUFFED BARLEY, STRAWBERRIES

SERVES 4

Disznoko, Tokaji, Late Harvest
(Hungary)

Ingredients

Puffed Barley
50g barley
oil (to deep fry)
icing sugar (to dust)

Whisky Set Cream
850ml cream
280ml whole milk
280ml whisky
280g icing sugar
2 sheets gelatine (soaked in cold water)

Strawberry Sorbet
1kg strawberry purée
2 tbsp glucose

Strawberries
1 punnet strawberries
caster sugar

Method

For The Puffed Barley (Prepare ahead)

Boil the barley until soft, then drain and dehydrate in a dehydrator (62°C) or very low oven for 24 hours. Deep fry and toss in icing sugar.

For The Whisky Set Cream (Prepare ahead)

Reduce the cream by one third, then leave to cool.

Warm the milk and whisky with the icing sugar and gelatine until the gelatine is melted. Leave to cool.

Ribbon whip the reduced cream, then fold all the ingredients together and set in a mould in the fridge for 4 hours.

For The Strawberry Sorbet

Bring the purée and glucose to the boil. Cool, then churn in an ice cream machine.

For The Strawberries

Lightly cover half the strawberries with sugar and place over a *bain-marie* until softened. Pass through a fine sieve and keep the liquid. Slice the remaining strawberries and dress in the liquid.

To Serve

Serve as pictured.

216

WEDGWOOD
THE RESTAURANT

267 Canongate, Royal Mile, Edinburgh, EH8 8BQ

0131 558 8737
www.wedgwoodtherestaurant.co.uk Twitter: @chefwedgwood
Facebook: Wedgwood the Restaurant Instagram: @chefwedgwood

Situated in the heart of Edinburgh's historic Old Town on the famous Royal Mile, Wedgwood the Restaurant has established itself as a firm favourite amongst Edinburgh locals and visitors alike. Chef Paul Wedgwood and his wife Lisa built the restaurant based on their vision of the perfect night out with relaxed, unhurried, friendly service, a great wine list, comfortable and stylish surroundings and fabulous food at the heart of it. It's proven to be a formula for success, winning awards on an annual basis and holding a Michelin listing since 2010.

The restaurant offers a special culinary experience to suit all palates and budgets, taking the very best ingredients that Scotland has to offer and elevating it to something truly unique and memorable, with twists and takes on classic dishes such as Paul's signature lobster thermidor crème brûlée. The restaurant is renowned for sourcing some of the most unusual wild ingredients and Paul can often be found foraging around the shores, woods and riverbanks near Edinburgh for that extra special something to lift his dishes to an exceptional level. You'll also find some classic dishes such as fillet and shin of Buccleuch beef, parsnips, carrots, marrow crumb, red wine jus and the popular VERY sticky toffee pudding, Caol Ila butterscotch with vanilla ice cream on the menu. And, not forgetting the award-winning international wine list which features Wedgwood's unique Rioja Reserva, hand-picked from the Altanza winery in Spain.

Wedgwood photography by Lewis Notarangelo

Offering a great value lunch menu as well as à la carte and the 'Wee Taste of Scotland' tasting menu at dinner, Wedgwood creates a memorable dining experience where every visit is an occasion.

PAN SEARED KING SCALLOPS, WHISKED CULLEN SKINK

SERVES 4

 FMC, Ken Forrester, Stellenbosch (South Africa)

Method

For The Pan Seared King Scallops

Remove the scallops from their shells, remove the coral, then cut the meat in half horizontally. Clean the shells and reserve for service. When ready to serve, cook the scallops in a hot frying pan to your liking.

Chef's Tip

Be ethically minded in your purchase of scallops; ask your fishmonger for hand-dived scallops, not dredged.

For The Whisked Cullen Skink

Gently fry the onion in the butter in a heavy-based saucepan until softening. Pour the milk into the pan, then add the bay leaf and potato and simmer for 10 minutes. Add the haddock and leek and simmer gently for 5 minutes.

Remove the fish and strain the sauce, reserving the vegetables. Using a stick blender, whisk the sauce until light and very frothy.

To Serve

Break up the fish and share between 4 scallop shells. Top the flaked fish with the reserved onion, diced potato and leek.

Serve 3 half scallops per shell on top of the leek and potato, then cover with the foam.

Ingredients

6 extra-large king scallops (in half shell)

Whisked Cullen Skink

15g butter
¼ onion (finely sliced)
150ml whole milk
1 bay leaf
1 medium Maris piper potato (peeled, diced into 75mm cube)
100g smoked haddock
1 leek (mid-section only, finely sliced)

ROSE VEAL, ALE BRAISED BARLEY, ONION, CABBAGE, SWEETBREADS

SERVES 4

 Fleurie, Domaine Lardy, Beaujolais (France)

Ingredients

Veal And Sweetbreads

4 x 160g rose veal sirloin steaks (room temperature)
50g butter (for basting)
100g sweetbreads
flour (for dusting), 1 egg
panko breadcrumbs
salt and pepper
oil (for deep frying)

Ale Braised Barley

250g barley
500ml Arran Blonde ale
1 clove garlic
2 sprigs thyme, salt

Roast Onions

30ml olive oil
50g unsalted butter
4 small onions (cut in half vertically)
1 sprig thyme
1 sprig rosemary
250ml chicken stock

Onion Purée

50ml olive oil
50ml water
3 white onions (peeled, finely sliced)
1 sprig thyme, 1 bay leaf
salt and white pepper

Crisp Onion Rings

1 small onion (peeled, cut into thin rings)
50ml milk
flour (with a pinch of salt and ground white pepper)
oil (for deep frying)

Cabbage

4 hispi cabbage leaves
butter, salt

Method

For The Veal And Sweetbreads

Add the steaks to a hot pan and cook to your liking. When nearly ready, add butter and heat until foaming. Using a spoon, baste the steaks repeatedly. Season and allow to rest somewhere warm.

Cut the sweetbreads into bite-sized pieces and *pane* with flour, egg, then panko breadcrumbs. Deep fry (180°C) until cooked and golden brown.

> **Chef's Tip**
> Make sure you rest your steaks for a minimum of the same time you cooked them for.

For The Ale Braised Barley (Prepare ahead)

Soak the barley with the ale, garlic and thyme overnight in a large, covered bowl.

Place the contents of the bowl into a heavy-based saucepan with a good pinch of salt and cook the barley on a rolling boil until soft, stirring often. Add water as required so as the barley does not stick to the pan.

For The Roast Onions

Preheat the oven to 180°C.

Heat the oil and butter in a pan, carefully place the onions in flat-side down and cook over a medium heat until golden brown. Add the herbs and turn up the heat a little. Cover the onions with a sheet of greaseproof paper and slowly add the stock. Place the pan into the oven for 10 minutes, then remove and take out the onions. Remove the skins.

For The Onion Purée

Gently warm the olive oil and water in a saucepan before adding the onions, thyme and bay leaf. Season with salt and cover with a lid. Cook on a low temperature until the onions are very soft but not coloured. Remove the herbs and discard. Transfer the softened onions to a food processor and blitz until very smooth.

For The Crisp Onion Rings

Dust the onion rings in flour, place in the milk, then back into the flour and deep fry (180°C) until golden and crispy.

For The Cabbage

Remove the stems and rip the cabbage leaves. Bring to the boil some salted water and *blanch* the leaves for 45 seconds. Refresh in ice water, then drain. Heat some butter in a pan until foaming and add the cabbage until reheated. Serve immediately.

To Serve

Serve as pictured.

CHOCOLATE BROWNIE, BEETROOT MOUSSE, CHERRY GEL, CHOCOLATE SORBET, CRUMB

SERVES 4

 Recioto della Valpolicella, Fiorato, Tommasi, Veneto (Italy)

Ingredients

Brownie And Crumb

160g butter
200g dark chocolate (70%)
220g golden caster sugar
3 eggs
1 egg yolk
60g plain flour (sieved)
60g cocoa powder
100g dark chocolate buttons (70%)

Beetroot Mousse

250g fresh beetroots (washed, stalks removed)
100g white chocolate
150ml whipping cream

Cherry Gel

150g puréed cherries
25g icing sugar
½g xanthan gum

Chocolate Sorbet

150g caster sugar
750ml water
300g dark chocolate (70%)
50ml kirsch

Garnish

chocolate shards
red vein sorrel

Swiss roll tin (greased, lined)
mousse mould

Method

For The Brownie And Crumb

Preheat the oven to 170°C.

Melt the butter and the dark chocolate separately. Whisk together the sugar and eggs. Add the melted butter and dark chocolate and stir well to combine. Add the sieved flour, cocoa powder and dark chocolate buttons, then pour into the prepared Swiss roll tin. Bake for 20–30 minutes. Once cooked, allow to cool slightly, then cut into small squares.

To make the crumb, take one piece of brownie and crumble onto a baking sheet. Return to the oven for around 25 minutes or until dry and crumbly.

> **Chef's Tip**
>
> Try adding chopped toasted hazelnuts or pistachios to the mix before baking for a great texture, flavour and a different colour in the brownie.

For The Beetroot Mousse

Preheat the oven to 200°C.

Wrap the beetroots in foil and roast for 45-55 minutes until tender. Unwrap, cool, then peel and chop. Blend until smooth.

Melt the white chocolate in a *bain-marie*. Set aside and cool slightly.

Whisk the cream until thickened, then fold in the chocolate, followed by the beetroot purée. Spoon into the mousse mould and keep in the refrigerator until needed.

For The Cherry Gel

Blitz together the puréed cherries and icing sugar with a stick blender, then slowly add the xanthan gum until the desired thickness is achieved.

For The Chocolate Sorbet

Combine the sugar with 150ml of water in a saucepan. Bring to the boil while whisking to dissolve the sugar. Remove from the heat and whisk in the chocolate until melted. Allow to cool slightly, then add the kirsch and remaining 600ml of water. Blitz until smooth with a stick blender. Churn the mixture in an ice cream machine.

To Serve

Serve as pictured, garnished with shards of chocolate and red vein sorrel.

226
RELISH SCOTLAND LARDER

BAKERY

CAMPBELL'S BAKERY LTD.
59 King Street, Crieff, Perthshire, PH7 3HB
T: 01764 652114

Established in 1830, Campbell's Bakery is Scotland's oldest independent family run craft bakery. As well as traditional Scottish favourites such as Scotch pies, oatcakes and shortbread, Campbell's Bakery also produces an inspired range of breads and cakes, including black olive ciabatta, carrot and linseed, granary cob, lemon and dill and pumpkin seed loaf.

BEVERAGES

BUNNAHABHAIN WHISKY
Burn Stewart Distillers Ltd
Bunnahabhain Distillery, Port Askaig,
Isle of Islay, PA46 7RP
www.bunnahabhain.com
Twitter: BunnahabhainWhisky - @Bunnahabhain

Bunnahabhain is the flagship malt Scotch whisky from Burn Stewart Distillers and is exported to over 30 countries globally.

TEASMITH GIN
Udny, Aberdeenshire
T: 01651 214 225
www.teasmithgin.com

A Scottish premium gin, Teasmith is distilled using a blend of finely curated botanicals, including hand picked Ceylon tea which creates a classic gin that is light on the palate with a distinct, crisp freshness.

TOBERMORY MALT WHISKY

Tobermory Distillery, Ledaig, Tobermory, Isle of Mull
T: 01688 302 645
www.tobermorymalt.com

Crafted, nurtured and aged by islanders since 1798, Tobermory is simply one of Mull's hidden gems. Each bottle has been rested on Mull awaiting its time and when bottled it becomes something which can only be described as treasure.

WOODWINTERS WINES AND WHISKIES LTD

16 Henderson Street, Bridge of Allan, Scotland, FK9 4HP
91 Newington Road, Edinburgh, EH9 1QW
T: 01786 834 894/0131 6672 760
Mon-Sat 10am-7pm, Sun 1pm-5pm

IWSC UK Independent Wine Merchant of the Year 2010 and IWC Scottish Wine Merchant of the Year 2006, 2207 and 2009.

DAIRY

CLARKS SPECIALITY FOODS

98/6 Eastfield Drive, Penicuik, EH26 8HJ
T: 01968 675 257
www.clarksfoods.co.uk

Artisan cheese and quality food supplier, Clarks is a gourmet's delight focussing on farmhouse and artisan cheese, supplying over 300 types of cheese from around the UK and Europe. Suppliers of many other quality products.

GRAHAM'S THE FAMILY DAIRY

Airthrey Kerse Farm, Henderson Street,
Bridge of Allan, FK9 4RW
T: 01786 833 206
www.grahamsfamilydairy.com

Scottish dairy products including milk, butter and cream from Graham's Scottish Dairies.

KATY RODGER'S ARTISAN DAIRY

Knockraich Farm, Fintry, Stirlingshire, G63 0LN
T: 01360 860 202
www.knockraich.com

A small family run dairy producing Scotland's finest natural yoghurts, crème fraiche, crowdie, ice creams and frozen yoghurt.

Winner of the Scotland Food and Drink 'Product of the Year 2012'.

MACKIE'S

www.mackies.co.uk

World class indulgency from a family farm in Scotland.

The Mackie family has been farming at Westertown farm since 1912 and Mackie's of Scotland is now a well-known Scottish food brand. Formerly a milk retail company, Mackie's began making ice cream in 1986. Since then, they have added to their expanding range of ice creams, now offering everyday indulgences in the form of potato crisps and chocolate. The new chocolate factory is in what was formerly the old tractor shed on the farm. You can expect the best in natural ingredients. Mackie's products are readily available on the high street.

FINE AND SPECIALITY FOODS

BLACK AND GOLD COLD PRESSED RAPESEED OIL
Stevenson Mains Farm, Haddington, East Lothian, EH41 4PU
T: 01620 826 670
www.blackandgoldoil.co.uk

The Elder family have farmed in East Lothian for over 150 years and have being sowing, growing, overseeing the pressing, harvesting and selling of their delicious cold pressed rapeseed oil for over 25 years. Available to buy online, as well as being sold in fine food outlets the length and breadth of the country.

JK FINE FOODS
16 Chattan Place, Aberdeen, AB10 6RD
T: 01224 580 778
www.jkfinefoods.co.uk

A local family run business, supplying fresh fish from Peterhead and championing local produce and suppliers.

LETTERFINLAY FINE FOODS
Units 1 & 2 Annat Industrial Estate, Corpach,
Fort William, PH33 7NA
T: 01397 772957

For meats and speciality goods.

MACKINTOSH OF GLENDAVENY
Glendaveny, Peterhead, Aberdeenshire, AB42 3E
T: 07876 474 546
www.mackintoshofglendaveny.co.uk

Extra virgin, cold pressed rapeseed oil, home grown, pressed and bottled in Aberdeenshire. 100% free from chemicals and preservatives.

STRATHSPEY MUSHROOMS
Unit 4 A3, Strathspey Industrial Estate, Woodlands Terrace,
Grantown on Spey, PH26 3NB
T: 01479 873 344
www.getdeli.co.uk

Wonderful Scottish mushrooms and deli products.

WALKERS SHORTBREAD

www.walkersshortbread.com

The Walkers story begins in 1898 when 21 year old Joseph Walker opened the doors of his own bakery with a loan of £50 and the ambition to bake 'The World's Finest Shortbread'. Now it is his grandchildren and great grandchildren who continue the tradition of fine baking that he started. Walkers shortbread is exported to over 60 countries around the world - all of it baked to the original recipe in the stunning Speyside region of the Scottish Highlands. The shortbread has won numerous international accolades including five gold Mondiale medals and the Food from Britain Innovation Award. Walkers products are readily available in supermarkets and independent delis alike, or online directly from Walkers.

FISH

AJ DUNCAN (DIVING SERVICES)
Leven
T: 07867 794 040

Supplier of hand-dived scallops.

ALFIE EDWARDS
Burnside, Camusterrach, Applecross, IV54 8LT
T: 01520 744 313

Alfie is a local fish supplier who can supply most fish, shellfish and local fruit and vegetables, all when in season. Van deliveries in a regulated chiller van.

DAVID LOWRIE
Fish Merchant
St Monan's
T: 01333 730 770

Supplier of fish and shellfish.

GEORGE CAMPBELL AND SON
Perth
T: 01738 638 454

Supplier of fish and shellfish.

ISLE OF MULL CRAB COMPANY
Croig, Dervaig, Isle of Mull
T: 01688 400 364
www.mullcrab.co.uk

A family business, now in its fourth generation, which has been trading since 1921. Suppliers of all types of fish, smoked fish, seafood and shellfish (fresh and frozen). Their specialities are their superb oak-smoked salmon and their dyed or undyed smoked haddock, smoked on the premises.

JAMES DICKSON AND SON, FISHMONGER AND CURER
West Harbour Road, Prestonpans, EH32 0HX
T: 01875 811 301

A small family-run business specialising in fresh hand-picked crab meat. The secret of Isle of Mull crab is the fresh quality of the crab as it is caught daily aboard the creel boat 'Eilean Ban'. Once caught, the best of the catch is selected to be hand-picked for the local market.

GOURLINE FISH MERCHANTS
West Quay, Gourdon, Montrose, Angus, DD10 0NA
T: 01561 361 545
www.gourline.co.uk

Fresh haddock, sole, plaice and cod caught by their own vessels and landed on their doorstep at West Quay allows them to ensure their fish are the freshest available.

In addition to their merchant service, they are pleased to offer a smoking facility - through a traditional kiln process. They smoke any form of seafood overnight.

HAND-DIVED HIGHLAND SHELLFISH
(Andrew Reid)
T: 07899 995 600
www.highlandshellfish.co.uk

Provide the best live scallops from the west coast. Dived for and delivered within 24 hours.

LOCH DUART SALMON
Badcall Salmon House, Scourie, Lairg,
Sutherland, IV27 4TH
T: 01670 660 161
www.lochduart.com

The difference begins with their approach to rearing salmon and ends with a product which is consistently judged superior in taste, quality, colour and overall perception, as evidenced by the number of international leading chefs and restaurants which service Loch Duart farmed salmon by name.

STEVE COOPER AT SRC FOODS

15 Ladysmith Street, Ullapool,
Ross-shire, IV26 2UW
T: 01854 613 020
www.srcfoods.com

*Independent seafood supplier and wholesaler based in
Ullapool on the west coast of the Highlands of Scotland -
home to some of the finest shellfish and seafood in
the world.*

TOBERMORY FISH FARM

Baliscate, Tobermory, Isle of Mull
T: 01688 302 120

TOSCAIG SHELLFISH (ALI MACLEOD)

The Schoolhouse, Applecross, IV54 8LT
T: 01520 744348
fishermanapx@btinternet.com

*Creel-caught Applecross Bay prawns and squat lobsters
orders taken subject to weather conditions.*

WILLIE-FISH

8 Stevenson Street, Oban, Argyll, Scotland, PA34 5NA
T: 01631 567 156
www.williefishoban.co.uk

*A wide range of seafood and shellfish, including scallops,
razor clams, oysters, smoked salmon and trout, as well as
smoked fish pâté. As far as possible, all their fish is sourced
locally but they are happy to track down any variety not
readily available.*

MEAT AND POULTRY

THE ABERFOYLE BUTCHER

206 Main Street, Aberfoyle, FK8 3UQ
T: 01877 382 473
www.aberfoylebutcher.co.uk

*An independent butcher cradled in the heart of the
Trossachs. They can supply directly to your kitchen, whether
it's an exquisite restaurant, hotel or if you simply appreciate
the finest food at home.*

APPLECROSS ESTATE LARDER
Applecross House, Applecross, IV54 8ND
T: 01520 744 247
www.applecrossestatetrust.org

Prime venison carcass, shot on the peninsula and hung in the larder until in prime condition.

BEL'S BUTCHER
25a High Street, Edzell, Angus, DD9 7TE
T: 01356 648 409

Excellent Angus beef and black pudding to meet your specific requirements.

BRAEHEAD FOODS
7 Moorfields North Industrial Park, Crosshouse, Kilmarnock KA2 0FE
T: 0156 550 008
www.braeheadfoods.co.uk

Leading purveyor of speciality foods and game.

GREAT GLEN GAME
The Old Butcher's Shop, Roy Bridge, PH33 4AE
T: 01397 712 121
www.greatglengame.co.uk

For wild venison and preserved meats.

JOHN ANDERSON BUTCHERS
36 High Street, North Berwick, EH39 4HQ
T: 01620 892 964

Award-winning butcher selling high-quality, locally sourced meat and game. Helpful staff able to offer advice. Suppliers to the public as well as to the food industry.

JOHN HENDERSON MEAT
Unit 8, Fife, Glenrothes, KY6 2RU
T: 01592 770 555
jhenderson@ic24.net

David and Andrew offer quality and customer care and are always keen to offer fresh ideas.

MACPHAIL'S ISLE OF MULL VENISON
Woodside Croft, Salen, Isle of Mull
T: 01680 300 220

SCOTCH LAMB PGI

www.qmsscotland.co.uk

What is Scotch Lamb PGI?

Nowadays it's only natural to want to know where your food comes from. However, we don't always have time to study the back of every packet we pick up. Luckily, when it comes to choosing fresh or frozen lamb: you can simply look for the label that says Scotch Lamb PGI to be sure of quality in every bite. The Quality Meat Scotland assurance logos are shorthand for wholesomeness, safety and taste. Only meat carrying the Scotch Lamb PGI logo is guaranteed to come from animals born and reared on assured Scottish farms. The PGI (Protected Geographical Indication) logo is your guarantee of a genuinely authentic product. Since 1996 Scotch Lamb has held the coveted European Protected Geographical Indication (PGI) status which legally protects it from imitation by meat from out with Scotland or from products claiming Scotch status. You can be sure that whenever you buy Scotch Lamb PGI that it's the genuine article. It has been quality assured for its whole life in Scotland; the farm and processor has been independently audited to make sure they meet stringent requirements regarding animal welfare and natural production methods. This all means that the Scotch Lamb you buy is fully traceable back to its farm of origin.

SMOKED FOODS

FEOCHAN MHOR SMOKEHOUSE
Kilmore, Oban, Argyll, PA34 4XT
T: 01631 770 670
www.feochanmhorsmokehouse.co.uk

Delicious smoked fish, pâtés and shellfish from the smokehouse. Also fresh fish and shellfish from their shop in Oban.

GALLOWAY SMOKEHOUSE
Carsluith, Newton Stewart, DG8 7DN
T: 01671 820 354
www.gallowaysmokehouse.co.uk

All foods are cured with salt before smoking and, to give a fuller flavour, they add dark syrup and black rum to the salmon. Their prize-winning smoked foods are a gourmet's delight.

VEGETABLES AND FRUIT

MARK MURPHY AND PARTNER LTD
Unit 2 Newbridge Industrial Estate,
Newbridge, Midlothian, EH28 8PJ
T: 0131 335 3040
www.markmurphyltd.co.uk
Facebook: /markmurphyltd.co.uk
Twitter: /markmurphyltd
enquiries@markmurphyltd.co.uk

Established in 1981 and now employs over 90 staff. Open all day, every day. Their large fleet of refrigerated vehicles deliver across Edinburgh, the Central Belt, the Borders and part of the Highlands.

Suppliers of premium quality fruit and vegetables, dairy products and fine foods, with a great deal of experience as well as a comprehensive understanding of the catering trade's requirements. Because they understand the catering trade, deliveries are made six days a week, with a back up supply on Sundays to Edinburgh City.

MACLEOD ORGANICS
Kylerona Farm, 8 Hillhead, Ardersier, IV2 7QZ
T: 01667 462 555
www.macleodorganics.co.uk

A family firm that has been delivering since October 1998 with a proud history. Fully committed to bringing the freshest, local and 100% organic products to your doorstep.

WILLIAMSON GROUP LTD
5 Walker Road, Longman Industrial Estate,
Inverness, IV1 1TD
T: 01463 236 600

Suppliers of fresh fruit, salad, vegetables, dairy, deli and dry goods. Will always help to source requirements. Good on local food.

235
RELISH READER OFFER

IF YOU LOVE FOOD, GETTING AWAY AND AMAZING READER OFFERS, THEN YOU'LL LOVE THIS...

In celebration of the launch of over 400,000 hotels available across the world on the charitablebookings.com lifestyle reservations platform, receive your FREE copy of Volume 3, the new hardback book from Charitable Bookings Signature Dish cookbook collection, including 250 recipes from a selection of the world's greatest chefs.

VOLUME 3 INCLUDES:

- 176 pages
- 83 full colour images
- 50 recipes across 100 pages
- 25 foodie facts and full 250 chef listing
- Unique code unlocking 250 recipes on the charitablebookings.com lifestyle app

- Weights and measurements bookmark
- Silk ribbon bookmark

In addition, you will also receive the chance to WIN five nights for two at the five star Anantara Kihavah Maldives including full board and sea plane transfers worth over £7500. Simply download the free **charitablebookings.com** lifestyle app and enter this **reader offer code: UM2222** to be entered into the FREE holiday draw and to receive your FREE cookbook for yourself to enjoy or to gift to a loved one.

For full terms and conditions and competition end date, see the charitablebookings.com lifestyle app.

GLOSSARY

AL DENTE
Al dente describes vegetables that are cooked to the 'tender crisp' phase - still offering resistance to the bite, but cooked through. Al dente can also describe cooked pasta which is firm but not hard.

BAIN-MARIE
A pan or other container of hot water with a bowl placed on top of it. This allows the steam from the water to heat the bowl so ingredients can be gently heated or melted.

BEURRE NOISETTE
Unsalted butter is melted over a low heat until it begins to caramelise and brown. When it turns a nutty colour, it should be removed from the heat to stop it burning.
Can be used as a base for butter sauces or added to cakes and batters.

BLANCH
Boiling an ingredient before removing it and plunging it in ice cold water in order to stop the cooking process.

BRUNOISE
A type of culinary cut in which food is diced into quarter inch (3.175mm) cubes. The formal-looking little squares add colour and elegance to dishes.

CARTOUCHE
A piece of greaseproof paper that covers the surface of a stew, soup, stock or sauce to reduce evaporation.

CHINOIS
A conical sieve with an extremely fine mesh. It is used to strain custards, purées, soups and sauces, producing a very smooth texture.

CLARIFIED BUTTER
Milk fat rendered from butter to separate the milk solids and water from the butter fat.

CONFIT
A method of cooking where the meat is cooked and submerged in a liquid to add flavour. Often this liquid is rendered fat. Confit can also apply to fruits - fruit confits are cooked and preserved in sugar, the result is like candied fruits.

DEGLAZE
To make a gravy or sauce by adding liquid to the cooking juices and food particles in a pan in which meat or other ingredients have been cooked.

EMULSION/EMULSIFY
In the culinary arts, an emulsion is a mixture of two liquids that would ordinarily not mix together, like oil and vinegar.

FRENCH TRIMMED

To French trim, fat, meat or skin is cut away to expose a piece of bone, so that it sticks out.

It also means that any excess fat is cut off. French Trimming can be done to lamb chops and bigger cuts; it can even can be done to chicken legs or breasts.

GASTRIQUE

A caramelised sugar, deglazed with vinegar, used as a flavouring for sauces.

JULIENNE

A culinary knife cut in which the vegetable is sliced into long thin strips, similar to matchsticks.

LIQUOR

The liquid that is left over from the cooking of meat or vegetables. Can be incorporated into sauces and gravy.

MACERATED

Raw, dried or preserved fruit and vegetables soaked in a liquid to soften the food or to absorb the flavour.

MIREPOIX

Finely diced combination of celery (pascal, celery or celeriac), onions and carrots. There are many regional mirepoix variations, which can sometimes be just one of these ingredients, or include additional spices creating a rich, flavoursome base to sauces or stews.

NAGE

A term for a flavoured liquid used for poaching delicate foods, typically seafood. A traditional nage is a broth flavoured with white wine, vegetables and herbs, in which seafood is poached. The liquid is then reduced and thickened with cream and/or butter.

PANE

To coat with flour, beaten egg and breadcrumbs for deep frying.

QUENELLE

A neat, three-sided oval (resembling a mini rugby ball) that is formed by gently smoothing the mixture between two dessertspoons.

ROCHER

A one-handed quenelle.

SABAYON

Made by beating egg yolks with a liquid over simmering water until thickened and increased in volume. The liquid can be water, but Champagne or wine is often used.

SAUTE

To fry in a small amount of fat.

SOUS VIDE

French for 'under vacuum.' A method of cooking food sealed in airtight plastic bags in a water bath or in a temperature-controlled steam environment for longer than normal cooking times. The intention is to cook the item evenly, ensuring that the inside is properly cooked without overcooking the outside, and to retain moisture.

ALL THE INGREDIENTS FOR YOUR RECIPE TO SUCCESS

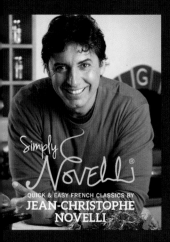

Relish is proud to have worked with more than 1500 of the UK's finest chefs to showcase their wonderful restaurants and food but there is a huge appetite for more.

Mark Greenaway and Jean Christophe Novelli are just two of the industry's leading lights who worked with our small, professional and dedicated team to produce their own beautiful books - stamped with their personality and signature dishes.

We are delighted and proud to share with you the news that Mark's book Perceptions was named the world's best chef cookbook at the Gourmand World Cookbook Awards 2017. It is an amazing accolade and testament to Mark's passion for the art and the wonderful natural larder he works with. Perceptions is an outstanding example of how, as an independent publisher, we are able to focus on you, your restaurant and your region to showcase culinary excellence to our readers who are always hungry to try out new dishes.

Owning this book is just for starters, reading it is the main course. Why not go for dessert and let us help you create a bespoke publication of your own to share with your loyal customers and attract new fans along the way? You will be on the shelves alongside our fantastic portfolio of beautifully illustrated guides, which are stocked nationally in Waterstones, Harvey Nichols, in each featured restaurant, in leading independent stores and online globally. You could be the next published chef to join the world's elite

Relish has a small, friendly, professional team, with experience in publishing, print management, editing, proofing, photography, design and artwork, sales distribution and marketing. We ensure a personal approach, working exceptionally hard to develop a great product which reflects each chef's talent and passion.

Duncan and Teresa Peters established the company in 2009, with a vision of building a niche publishing house for food lovers. The success of Relish Publications is reflected in the fact that we are the UK's leading regional recipe book publisher.

To book a personal consultation with our friendly, dedicated team contact our head office on 01670 517 635.

"Relish books are full of enjoyable recipes and ideas for making the most of the edible treasures we have on our doorstep; both places to eat them and new, exciting ways to cook them."

Angela Hartnett, MBE

"The Relish cookbook offers the home cook some great inspiration to make the most of these wonderful ingredients in season."

Tom Kitchin

"With mouth-watering, easy to follow recipes and beautiful photography, this book is a must have for any foodie, from professional chef to the inspired home cook."

Michael Caines MBE

"The North East and Yorkshire has an amazing food and drink scene with a fantastic array of produce and restaurants - available on your doorstep. Relish gives you a taste of what we all have to offer through the pages of this superb book."

Kenny Atkinson

"Relish Midlands is a fantastic recipe book that brings together so many of the talented chefs and quality restaurants in the area. It gives you a taste of what our exciting region has to offer as well as the encouragement to try some new recipes."

Adam Stokes

"Relish Wales is a fabulous way to showcase some of our beautiful country's fabulous eateries and to be able to share our food with a wider audience."

Stephen Terry

AVAILABLE TO BUY IN OUR FEATURED RESTAURANTS & IN ALL GOOD BOOKSHOPS

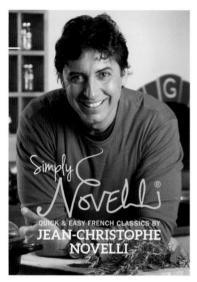

Simply Novelli®
QUICK & EASY FRENCH CLASSICS BY JEAN-CHRISTOPHE NOVELLI

Mark Greenaway

PERCEPTIONS
RECIPES FROM RESTAURANT MARK GREENAWAY

Dip in Brilliant
An Indian recipe adventure with a contemporary twist

By Dipna Anand
Foreword by Michel Roux Junior

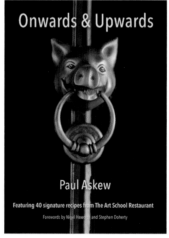

Onwards & Upwards

Paul Askew

Featuring 40 signature recipes from The Art School Restaurant
Forewords by Nigel Haworth and Stephen Doherty

Relish
SOUTH EAST
Original recipes from the region's finest chefs and restaurants.
Introduction by Angela Hartnett, MBE.

Relish
NORTH EAST & YORKSHIRE
SECOND HELPING
Original recipes from the North East and
Yorkshire's finest chefs and restaurants.
Introduction by Kenny Atkinson.

Relish
SOUTH WEST
SECOND HELPING
Original recipes from the South West's
finest chefs and restaurants.
Introduction by chef Nathan Outlaw.

THIRD EDITION

Relish
WALES
Original recipes from the region's
finest chefs and restaurants.
Introduction by chef Will Holland.

Relish
NORTH WEST
SECOND HELPING
Original recipes from the region's
finest chefs and restaurants.
Introduction by chef Paul Askew.

Relish
MIDLANDS
SECOND HELPING
Original recipes from the region's finest chefs
and restaurants. Introduction by Adam Stokes.

Relish
SCOTLAND
THIRD HELPING
Original recipes from the region's finest chefs
and restaurants. Featuring the Michelin starred
chefs of Scotland.

242
HINTS & TIPS

HOW TO MAKE ICE CREAM WITHOUT A MACHINE

Although relatively inexpensive these days, not everyone has access to an ice cream machine. That's no reason not to follow some of these delicious recipes found in the Relish Scotland book. Although more time consuming than a machine, excellent results can be obtained by following this simple method.

Follow the recipe right up until it tells you to churn in the machine, including any chilling time in the fridge.

Take your mixture from the fridge and stir with a rubber spatula. Transfer it to a suitable plastic container with a lid. There should be at least 2cm space at the top to allow the mixture to expand when freezing. Cover and place in the freezer for two hours.

Remove from the freezer and beat with a hand mixer, still in the container, to break up the ice crystals that are beginning to form. Cover and return to the freezer for a further 2 hours. (If you don't have a hand mixer then you may use a fork and some 'elbow grease' to break up the crystals).

Remove from the freezer and beat again with the hand mixer. The ice cream should be thickening up nicely at this point but too soft to scoop. Return it to the freezer for an additional hour. Beat again. If your ice cream is still not thickened sufficiently, repeat this process again after another hour. When the ice cream has thickened properly, stir in any add-ins at this point (honeycomb, nuts...). Do not beat with the hand mixer after the add-ins have been mixed in.

Place the tightly sealed container in the freezer and allow the ice cream to freeze until firm. The ice cream should be removed from the freezer 15-20 minutes before you wish to eat it. This will make scooping easier.

This method will also work for sorbets. Sometimes sorbets may go a bit 'icy' or 'crumbly' if left for too long in the freezer. This can be rectified by blitzing in a food processor just before serving.

Sticky Toffee Pudding, Butterscotch Sauce - **Page 44**

HOW TO MAKE A SUGAR STOCK SYRUP

This makes about 750ml stock syrup. It can be stored in a sterilised jar in the fridge for a couple of months.

500g white sugar
500ml water

Place the sugar and water in a pan. Dissolve slowly over a very low heat. You must not allow the syrup to boil until all the sugar has dissolved, about 5 minutes. Once completely dissolved, bring to the boil, then simmer for 5 minutes.

CONVERSION CHART

COOKING TEMPERATURES

Degrees Celsius	Fahrenheit	Gas Mark
140	275	1
150	300	2
160-170	325	3
180	350	4
190	375	5
200-210	400	6
220	425	7
230	450	8
240	475	9

*Temperatures for fan-assisted ovens are, as a general rule, normally about 20°C lower than regular oven temperatures.

WEIGHT MEASUREMENT CONVERSIONS

1 teaspoon (5ml/5g)	$1/4$ oz
1 tablespoon (15ml/15g)	$3/4$ oz
10g	$1/2$ oz
25g	1oz
50g	2oz
75g	3oz
150g	5oz
200g	7oz
250g	9oz
350g	12oz
450g	1lb
1kg	2.2lb

VOLUME MEASUREMENT CONVERSIONS

55ml	2 fl oz
150ml	$1/4$ pt
275ml	$1/2$ pt
570ml	1 pt
1 litre	$1^3/4$ pt